DOSTOEVSKY AND SUICIDE

AF860613

DOSTOEVSKY AND SUICIDE

N.N. SHNEIDMAN
UNIVERSITY OF TORONTO

MOSAIC PRESS
OAKVILLE NEW YORK LONDON

Canadian Cataloguing in Publication Data

Schneidman, N.N.
Dostoevsky and suicide

ISBN 0-88962-244-2 (bound). - ISBN 0-88962-243-4 (pbk.)

1. Dostoevsky, Fyodor, 1821-1881 - Criticism and interpretation. 2. Suicide in literature. I. Title.

PG3328.Z7S95 1984 891.73'3 C84-099428-1

No part of this book may be reproduced or transmitted in any form, by any means, electronic or mechanical, including photocopying and recording, information storage and retrieval systems, without permission in writing from the publisher, except by a reviewer who may quote brief passages in a review.

Published by Mosaic Press, P.O. Box 1032, Oakville, Ontario, L6J 5E9, Canada. Offices and warehouse at 1252 Speers Road, Unit 10, Oakville, Ontario, L6L 5N9, Canada.

Published with the assistance of the Canada Council and the Ontario Arts Council; and, with the help of a grant from the Canadian Federation for the Humanities using funds provided by the Social Sciences and Humanities Research Council of Canada.

Copyright©N.N. Shneidman, 1984
Design by Doug Frank
Typeset by Speed River Graphics
Printed and bound in Canada.

ISBN 0-88962-244-2 cloth
ISBN 0-88962-243-4 paper

MOSAIC PRESS:
In the United States:
Flatiron Book Distributors, 175 Fifth Avenue, Suite 814, New York, N.Y. 10010, U.S.A.
In the U.K.:
John Calder (Publishers) Ltd., 18 Brewer Street, London, W1R 4As, England.
In New Zealand & Australia:
Pilgrims South Press, P.O. Box 5101, Dunedin, New Zealand.

TABLE OF CONTENTS

PREFACE

Dostoevsky, one of the great nineteenth century Russian novelists, has received exhaustive treatment in literary criticism. Surprisingly, in spite of Dostoevsky's extensive investigation of self-destruction and the frequent depiction of suicide in his prose, there is, as yet, no single study devoted to the detailed discussion of these problems in his works. That does not mean, of course, that individual suicides in Dostoevsky's novels have not been dealt with by literary historians and critics. To the contrary, much attention has been devoted to the discussion of his "logical" suicides, but considerably less emphasis has been placed on the interpretation and analysis of the suicides of other important characters.

This study has been prompted by the desire to fill the existing gap in Dostoevsky scholarship by analyzing interpreting and classifying all suicides in his creative and journalistic writings. It begins with an investigation of the destructive and self-destructive elements prevalent in the natures of Dostoevsky's early heroes because I believe that there is a close connection between the irrational self-destructive tendencies exhibited by these characters and the violent acts of suicide in his mature fiction. The transition from self-destructive behaviour to the violent murder of self in the later novels has been influenced by Dostoevsky's personal experience in Siberia and by a new emphasis on the dramatic qualities of his art. Thus his early works could be regarded as the creative laboratory for his major novels.

Dostoevsky's art is multilevelled, a fact which makes difficult a unidimensional approach to his fiction and which leads, in turn, to the use of different methods of analysis to elucidate the meaning of different suicides in his works. To that end I analyse the artistic relevance of suicide in Dostoevsky's novels within the context of the works discussed as well as within the broader spectrum of the psychological and social sciences in order that we may understand better the subconscious motives which often guide man in his actions. Finally, I make an attempt to draw certain conclusions which help to determine the function and the general significance of suicide in the works of Dostoevsky.

The first chapter discusses suicide as a general human phenomenon. In the following chapters Dostoevsky's works are examined in chronological order. For that reason "The Eternal Husband" (*Vechnyi muzh*, 1870), although a minor work, appears in the chapter dealing with Dostoevsky's major works of fiction.

When first mentioned, the title of a work by Dostoevsky is given in English, with the original title and date of publication in parentheses. Subsequently, the titles of these works are given in English only. I have adopted here the widely used transliteration system of the Library of Congress with a minor modification in the spelling endings of Russian surnames. In quotations from English sources the original transliteration is preserved.

I would like to use this opportunity to express my gratitude to all those who encouraged and helped me in the course of my work on this book. I am indebted to Professor K.A. Lantz and to my daughter, Rose, who have read the manuscript and offered constructive criticism.

This book has been published with the help of a grant from the Canadian

Federation for the Humanities, using funds provided by the Social Sciences and Humanities Research Council of Canada.

I gratefully acknowledge the assistance of different institutions and the help and advice of my colleagues and friends, but I accept sole responsibility for any inaccuracies and mistakes that may exist in this book.

N.N.S.

Toronto, Canada

I. INTRODUCTION: SUICIDE IN LIFE AND FICTION

Death is a fact of the human condition. It is a reality which is part of our daily existence. Death is both a personal matter, arousing sorrow and despair and a social phenomenon with wide ranging psychological, philosophical, sociological and often, political implications. Man begins to die from the very day of his birth. All his conscious life he attempts to come to terms with the inevitability of his own demise. He tries to prepare himself for death, but his efforts are futile because he is seldom ready to part with his life. Man's life and activities are often determined by his attitude to death, by his faith or lack of it, by his belief in personal immortality or by his scepticism about the existence of a future life.

Death in Literature

The subject of literature is man and life in its entirety; no great artist could avoid dealing with the problem of death in his works. Russian classical literature is no exception to this rule. Different Russian writers, however, approach the subject of death from different perspectives. Thus, for example, little attention has been paid to the study of death and of the dying in the works of the prominent nineteenth century Russian writer N. Gogol'. The death of his protagonists in works such as "The Portrait" (1835) and "Vii" (1835) is placed in a fantastic setting. The title of his masterpiece, *Dead Souls* (1842), refers to metaphorical, symbolic, and spiritual death rather than to the actual death of real characters, depicted on the pages of the narrative.

In I. Turgenev's novel *Fathers and Sons* (1862) the death of the main character, Bazarov, is a fact not determined by the hero's life experience; it is rather, a reality which sheds light on the essence of his past. In stories such as "Death" (1848) or "Living Relics" (1874), Turgenev contemplates the death of the simple Russian peasant. He is amazed by the peasant's submissive acceptance of fate. But Turgenev does not investigate the psychology of the dying; instead, he observes the external manifestations of death and records his personal perception of this unfathomable phenomenon.

In the works of L. Tolstoy death is in most cases a conclusion of a natural life process which is often followed by the beginning of a new life which affirms the infinite process of procreation and eternal existence. Tolstoy's heroes *live*, however, until they breathe their last. Tolstoy dissects his dying heroes both physically and psychologically. The reader can easily identify with the spiritual suffering of Andrei Bolkonsky (*War and Peace*, 1869) or with the physical pain and anguish of Ivan Il'ich ("The Death of Ivan Il'ich" 1886). Tolstoy does not restrict himself to telling us about the death of his protagonists; he portrays the actual process of dying, showing that man's activity and life experience are closely intertwined with the way he faces death.

A. Chekhov, a physician with first-hand knowledge of the sick and the dying, deals in his stories and plays with different aspects of death. Some of his heroes are either murdered or kill themselves, while others die due to natural causes. But Chekhov restrains his own commentaries on the death of his heroes. He lets the facts speak for themselves. Thus, facing death, Bishop Petr ("The Bishop" 1902) realizes the emptiness and triviality of the concerns of those who are alive and well and not threatened yet by death. The approaching deaths of the embittered intellectual Pavel Ivanych and the peasant Gusev ("Gusev" 1890) symbolize man's extreme attitudes to life. The first rebels against life and refuses to accept death, while the latter submits passively to the inexorable powers of nature and fate. Death in Chekhov is a reality of human existence which reflects in a way on the lives not only of the departing, but also of those who are spared for the time beging from this inevitability.

Many deaths are recorded in the works of Dostoevsky. Beginning with the *Poor People* (*Bednye liudi*, 1846), there is hardly a significant work in which the life drama of a leading protagonist does not culminate in death. In each of Dostoevsky's major novels, including *Crime and Punishment* (*Prestuplenie i nakazanie*, 1866) and *The Brothers Karamazov* (*Brat'ia Karamazovy*, 1880), close to a dozen deaths are mentioned. Dostoevsky's novels are about vice and virtue, about saints and criminals, and very few protagonists in his novels die a natural death. Most deaths in his novels are the result of violent intrusion in the natural process of human life. All four of his major novels are essentially murder stories. At the heart of *Crime and Punishment* is murder for an idea. In *The Idiot* (*Idiot*, 1868) murder is the result of carnal passion. *The Possessed* (*Besy*, 1872) deals with political murder, while the subject of *The Brothers Karamazov* is parricide. In the few instances that important characters die a natural death, Dostoevsky mentions the reasons for their demise only in passing or fails to disclose them at all. Thus, for example, even though the death of the elder Zossima (*The Brothers Karamazov*) is described in some detail, we remain unaware of the actual medical problem which causes his demise.

A close scrutiny of Dostoevsky's artistic treatment of death suggests that his approach to this subject is different from that of most other Russian classical writers. Dostoevsky never deals with death as a biological problem of human life nor does he describe the physiological aspects of death. That is to say, death is seldom presented in Dostoevsky as an expression of the inexorable law of biological existence.[1] V.I. Kaigorodov suggests the ultimate reason for most deaths in Dostoevsky's fiction is "the violation of ethical rules by man himself, or by those who can influence his fate."[2] Thus it appears that the deaths of Dostoevsky's important protagonists are ethical symbols of major significance which are charged with ideological meaning relevant for the understanding and interpretation of his novels. Many of Dostoevsky's major characters embody ideas in action; the failure of an idea may often lead to the destruction of a hero, just as the death of a protagonist may signify the bankruptcy of his ideas.

Dostoevsky and Suicide

According to L. Grossman the composition of Dostoevsky's novels "can be reduced to two basic principles: significance of philosophical idea and interest of external intrigue... [which are] to compensate the reader for the tiring tension caused by his attention to the philosophical pages."[3] The ideological depth and dramatic intensity of Dostoevsky's novels always go hand in hand with the writer's ability to play on the readers' curiosity and his skill to keep the reader in a state of continuous suspense. Abrupt changes in the fortunes of man, instantateous decisions and actions fraught with unexpected consequences and violent death caused by murder or suicide, are some of the devices applied successfully by Dostoevsky with the purpose of rendering a philosophical or ethical message and keeping the readers' attention on the subject of the narrative.

Abrupt forceful termination of life is a device well fitting with the dramatic essence of Dostoevsky's art. Suicide, the ultimate means of self-destruction, is one of such devices. Indeed, as any great artist Dostoevsky could not avoid dealing with a problem as important as death and self-destruction. Yet it may appear that Dostoevsky is obsessed with the subject of suicide. Fourteen suicides are discussed or mentioned in Dostoevsky's five major novels, and a number of characters attempt or contemplate self-destruction. Alfred Alvarez, the author of a fascinating study of suicide in literature and himself an unsuccessful suicide, asks a pointed question: "But why this intensity, this need to nag away at the problem like a man enraged by a bad tooth? It may be that he [Dostoevsky] found suicide a greater temptation than he would have wished to acknowledge: but that is impossible to tell."[4]

A. Steinberg compares the your Dostoevsky with the eighteen-year-old Ippolit (*The Idiot*) and suggests that Ippolit's attempted suicide and his "Explanation" are saturated with autobiographical material. Drawing on the parallels between the "Explanation" and the young Dostoevsky's life experience, Steinberg asserts that "any biographer would have reason to assume that young Dostoievsky was then near suicide."[5] In fact it is possible to suggest that Dostoevsky shared some common traits with several of his suicides. Kirillov (*The Possessed*) and Smerdiakov (*The Brothers Karamozov*) have epilepsy, a disease afflicting their creator. Yet in all his writings Dostoevsky refers only a few times to his own possible self-destruction.

In a letter to his brother Mikhail, dated May 4, 1845, the young Dostoevsky threatens to kill himself if his novel *Poor People* does not pass the censor. He writes: "If I can't publish the novel I shall probably go into the Neva. What else *should* I do? I have thought of every single thing. I could not survive the death of my fixed idea."[6] On another occasion, in a letter to his friend A.E. Vrangel', sent from Semipolatinsk, and dated March 23, 1856, Dostoevsky expresses despair of the danger of losing his beloved future wife, and he exclaims "I will perish if I lose my angel: I will become mad, or I will go into the Irtysh [river]."[7]

It is doubtful whether the above statements could be taken as serious threats of suicide by the young author. Certainly, the mature Dostoevsky has no wish to die; his thirst for life is insatiable. In a note for the album of O. Kozlova, dated January 31, 1873, he writes: "I love life dearly. I love it for life's sake and I am still getting ready to begin my life seriously. I will soon be fifty and I still am unable to discern whether my life draws to an end or whether it is just at its beginning."[8] While it is possible to surmise that one's love of life does not necessarily exclude the possibility of suicide, nevertheless Dostoevsky's interest in the subject of suicide does not appear to be of a personal nature, that is, it is not the result of his preoccupation with problems of his own self-destruction. Dostoevsky, the writer, is aware of the great artistic potentialities of the theme of self-destruction in literature. He follows in the steps of his predecessors and contemporaries by making extensive use of this subject in his creative work.

Suicide in Literature

Dostoevsky is not the first nor the only writer to make use of suicide as an artistic device. In eight works by Shakespeare, for example, there are fourteen suicides.[9] Romeo and Juliet, Brutus, Cassius, Cleopatra, Antony, Othello, all kill themselves for different reasons. Close to four centuries have passed since Shakespeare created his masterpieces yet there is still no unanimity in the interpretation of the playwright's use of the motive of suicide. J.C. Collins propounds an idea that in no case is suicide in Shakespeare "associated with honor, but in all cases with intemperance or ignominy, or with both."[10] J.H. Hanford, on the other hand, contradicts the above assertion by claiming that Shakespeare's heroes " inflict death on themselves in a mood of exhilaration, with a strong consciousness of their own courage, and a sense of final triumph over the forces which have baffled and ruined them in life."[11] According to Hanford, Shakespeare's attitude toward suicide implies no moral theory and is determined wholly by the laws of art. We may suppose that "the dramatist was interested in the ethical problem of man's right to end his wretchedness or to forestall disgrace by seeking his own death. But what Shakespeare chiefly saw in this tremendous theme was material for tragedy."[12] Shakespeare is first of all a practicing dramatist who remains neutral and pragmatic in his attitude to moral problems and to the selection of sources, and "his own religious prejudices — whatever they might have been — were never allowed to subvert his instinct for practical dramatic effectiveness."[13]

Closer to Dostoevsky's own time the subject of suicide constitutes an important component of the sentimental novel, of romantic art, as well as of nineteenth century realism in literature. In the sentimental novel, where virtuous characters are often placed in pathetic situations, we often witness the culmination of human drama in suicide. Most famous in this respect is J.W. Goethe's Werther, who has been driven to suicide by unrequited love. *The Sorrows of Young Werther* (1774) was inspired by the suicide of a young diplomat with whom "Goethe himself could sympathize, even empathize, with his character."[14] It has been claimed by many that the publication of Goethe's novel "is said to have caused a wave of youthful suicides"[15], a fact highly disputed by some authorities on the problems of suicide. Jacques Choron is blunt in asserting that "Werther should not be taken as an approbation of suicide and even less as an apology for it. It is also a mistake to attribute to its influence a worldwide 'epidemic' of suicides, for the simple reason that no such epidemic occurred."[16]

The nineteenth century realistic novel, in particular the French one, abounds in dramatic conflicts culminating in acts of self-destruction. There are twenty-one suicides in the works of H. Balzac.[17] Emma, Gustave Flaubert's heroine in *Madame Bovary* (1857), is unable to live with her transgression and guilt and she poisons herself. Javert, in Victor Hugo's *Les Misérables* (1862), kills himself. Russian literature is not far behind. N. Karamzin's *Poor Liza* (1792) is very much in the tradition of *The Sorrows of*

Young Werther. Liza, Karamzin's young innocent heroine, throws herself into a deep pond after having realized that she has been forsaken by the man she loves. One of Turgenev's strong women, the proud Klara Milich (*Klara Milich*, 1883) cannot accept the indifference of the man she loves and she poisons herself. The young Katerina, in A. Ostrovsky's play "The Storm" (1859), cannot love her weak husband nor can she accept the tyrannical atmosphere reigning Russia's merchant life, and she is driven to suicide by her evil mother-in-law.

Even the young Tolstoy whose commitment to, and faith in life is at this time still overpowering, concludes one of his early stories "The Notes of a Billiard Marker" (1855) with a suicide. The young Nekhliudov squanders all his money and shoots himself. In another story, "Polikushka" (1863), a simple peasant loses his mistress' money and hangs himself in despair. The mature Tolstoy himself passes through a suicidal crisis before his religious conversion. Failing to grasp the meaning of life he contemplates self-destruction. Tolstoy writes in his *Confession* (1882): "It had come to this, that I, a healthy, fortunate man, felt I could no longer live: some irresistable power impelled me to rid myself one way or other of life. I cannot say I *wished* to kill myself. The power which drew me away from life was stronger, fuller, and more widespread than any mere wish. It was a force similar to the former striving to live, only in a contrary direction."[18] Tolstoy's spiritual tribulations and anguish are recreated in the character of Levin in *Anna Karenina* (1878). Levin's failure to comprehend the meaning of his existence brings him to the verge of suicide. Levin contemplates self-destruction. Vronsky attempts suicide by shooting himself, while Anna actually kills herself by jumping under the wheels of a running train.

It is evident that Dostoevsky's preoccupation with the subject of suicide is in line with the main literary tradition of his century. It is also well known that Dostoevsky's creative output has influenced the work and ideas of a number of twentieth century writers and thinkers, in particular, Franz Kafka, Hermann Hesse and Albert Camus. The characters created by these writers are blood relations of Dostoevsky's protagonists. They are ambivalent, mysterious, and irrational. They are trapped in a web of internal contradictions, unable to solve the disparity between the vagaries of their own natures and the realities of the external world. Joseph K., the guilt ridden hero of Kafka's *The Trial* (1925), is torn apart between his self-destructive sense of culpability and his desire to live. Seconds before his execution Mr. K. "knew perfectly well that it was his duty to grasp the knife himself as it passed from hand to hand above him, and to plunge it into himself. However, he did not do so, instead he turned his neck, which was still free, and looked about him ... the responsibility for this last failure lay with whoever had denied him the remnant of strength necessary for this deed."[19] Just like Dostoevsky's Ippolit, Joseph K. wants to rebel against irrational fate. He thinks of suicide as the last independent act he can commit as a free man. But his will to live is much stronger than the power of his rebellion. He is too weak to be able to put his ideas into action. His logic, that suicide is the only path available to an individual who wants to assert his freedom and to revolt against the injustice of fate, "may indeed be unshakeable, but it cannot withstand a man who is determined to live."[20]

Harry Haller, an avid reader of Dostoevsky and the main protagonist of Hesse's *Steppenwolf* (1929), is another recluse — a modern underground man. He is an intellectual who refuses to accept the corruption prevailing in his society and the imperfection of the world of which he is a part. He seeks solitude which gives him independence, but he fails to find within himself the contentment he searches for. He realizes that his new freedom is at the same time his death, because he stands all alone in a world rejected by him: "Haller belongs to those who have been caught between two ages, who are outside of all security and simple acquiescence. He belongs to those whose fate is to live the whole riddle of human destiny heightened to the pitch of a personal torture, a personal hell."[21] Haller contemplates suicide. He appoints his fiftieth birthday as the day on which to allow himself to take his own life. He admits that it is hard to hang oneself, "but to live is far, far harder,"[22] and yet he is condemned to live.

Meursault, the main protagonist of Camus' *The Stranger* (1946), is also condemned to die. He is a murderer. He is condemned to death, however, not only because he is a criminal but also because he is an outcast who refuses to conform to accepted social norms and conventions. Meursault acts on impulse, he refuses to pretend. His nature expresses the extreme dichotomy of body and mind, between the rational and irrational instincts guiding man's actions. He is indifferent to the external world, to life itself. He thinks that "it's common knowledge that life isn't worth living... it makes little difference whether one dies at the age of thirty or threescore and ten."[23] Meursault's predicament affirms the essential loneliness of man and the danger of being different. It confirms the self-destructive essence of man's inability to submit to social pressures. Finally, it illustrates that once the subtle balance in the relationship between man and society has been shattered, society rejects the individual, dooming him to spiritual desolation and physical destruction.

Suicide in Nineteenth Century Russia

Dostoevsky's interest in the problem of suicide is further enhanced by the realities of contemporary Russian life. Dostoevsky, the creative artist, perceptive observer of his milieu and an assiduous student of the lives of the members of the lower strata of Russian society (the downtrodden, the insulted and the injured) could not help but react to such a burning social phenomenon as suicide. Dostoevsky's attention to this problem was influenced by the ever-increasing growth in the rate of suicide in the rapidly changing Russia of the second half of the nineteenth century.

It is worthwhile to note that in the period between 1819 and 1875 the number of suicides in Russia increased from 17.6 to 29 per one million population.[24] This was mostly evident in Russia's western provinces, in particular in the city of Petersburg. Every month from twelve to fifteen people killed themselves in the capital. In 1870 there were 125 suicides in Petersburg, in 1871 there were 152 and in 1872 the figure had risen to 167.[25] In the years 1876, 1877 and 1878 there were in Petersburg on average 136 suicides per million people.[26] The number of suicides among men in Russia was much higher than that among women. In the years between 1870 and 1873 only from 19.6 to 20.4 per cent of all those who killed themselves were women. The rate of suicide increased with age and suicides among children occurred relatively seldom. Between the years 1869 and 1878 fifty-seven children between the ages of eight and sixteen committed suicide in Petersburg. In the same period in Moscow forty children killed themselves.[27] (It is interesting to note that the national suicide rate in Russia was lower and did not grow as fast as it did in the West. In the years 1871-75 the average number of suicides per year in eleven West European countries reached 118 per one million inhabitants. In the years 1876-80, the average was 150.[28] The number of suicides in Petersburg between the years 1875 and 1878 was higher than the national average by 263 per cent.[29] It is possible only to surmise that many suicides were the result of social pressure connected with post-reform industrialization and urbanization in Russia. According to the noted French sociologist Emile Durkheim, suicide exhibits all the characteristic traits of alienation in a society in which old family ties and religious and social foundations have been shattered. The individual is unable to cope with the sudden changes in his social position nor is he capable of integrating fully in a society which changes rapidly.[30]

Self-destruction and Self-preservation

For Dostoevsky suicide and self-destruction are not simply sociological problems connected with the lowly economic or social position of those concerned; many suicides in Dostoevsky are well-to-do people. Svidrigailov (*Crime and Punishment*), squanders his money before shooting himself. Stavrogin (*The Possessed*) is heir to his mother's estate but his financial solvency does not stop him from hanging himself.

Most suicides in Dostoevsky manifest the extreme complexity of human nature in which no single answer can supply an all-embracing justification for the behavioural patterns of man. Man's actions are often determined by two polar and contradictory traits of nature. On the one hand, man is driven by the natural instinct of self-preservation; on the other hand, his actions are often induced by the irrational impulse of self-destruction. According to Arthur Schopenhauer the will-to-live "is incapable of further explanation, but is the basis for every explanation ... it is the most real thing we know, in fact the kernel of reality itself."[31]

In a paper written in 1916, the Russian psycho-physiologist Ivan Pavlov declared that "all life is the fulfillment of a single aim, namely the preservation of life; it is the unceasing activity of what is commonly called the life instinct."[32] According to Pavlov this instinct takes the form of the goal reflex which motivates man's activity. Life is full and strong only in those who strive all their life towards some goal even though it is not always completely attainable.

Sigmund Freud, the father of the psychological explanation of suicide, offers many valuable insights to the understanding of man's self-destructive impulses which are in a paradoxical contradiction to the axiom that self-preservation is the first law of life. Freud's theory of suicide passes through several stages of evolutionary change. As late as 1910 Freud still questions as to "how it becomes possible for the extraordinary powerful life instinct to be overcome; whether this can only come about with the help of a disappointed libido or whether the ego can renounce its self-preservation for its own egoistic motives."[33] At this point Freud suspends his judgement on the subject of suicide until experience could help solve this problem. Ten years later Freud is "ready to assume the existence of only two basic instincts. *Eros* and the *destructive instinct.* The aim of the first of these basic instincts is to establish even greater unities and to preserve them thus — in short to bind together; the aim of the second is, on the contrary, to undo connections and so to destroy things. In the case of the destructive instinct, we may suppose that its final aim is to lead what is living into an organic state. For this reason we call it the *death instinct.*"[34]

Reasons for Suicide

The psychoanalytic explanations of the psychopathology of suicide are complex and sometimes ambiguous but they usually emphasize the fact that suicide is by no means a homogeneous or unitary piece of human behaviour and that it is determined by the interaction of several different motives. According to Freud there are

> "*general features* of the human condition, at least in Western civilization, that make each individual person somewhat vulnerable to suicide. These general features include: 1) the death instinct... 2) the splitting of the ego... 3) the group institutions, family and civilization, which require guilty compliance from every member of the group.... Individual suicides involve certain *specific suicide mechanisms.* All of them involve a breaking down of ego defences and the release of increased destructive energy. Examples are: 1) loss of love object.... 2) narcissistic injury.... 3) overwhelming affect: rage, guilt, anxiety, or combination; 4) extreme splitting of the ego... 5) a special suicidal attitude based on identification with someone who was suicidal."[35]

Thus it appears that suicide is a voluntary death, determined by a number of internal and external causes and often triggered by an upset to the healthy balance between the instincts of self-preservation and self-destruction in man.

Suicide can also be seen as a murder committed by the self. It is a death in which the murderer and the murdered are one and the same person. As the Freudian analyst Karl A. Menninger suggests: "probably no suicide is consummated unless — in addition to this wish to kill and to be killed — the suicidal person also wishes to die. Paradoxically many suicides in spite of the violence of the attack upon themselves and in spite of the corresponding surrender do not seem to be very eager to die."[36] This is perhaps the reason why "suicide is seldom committed out of reflection. It frequently happens that one event, often unimportant in itself, is just enough to precipitate the unconsciously borne rancor and all the boredom which had been held in suspension for a long time."[37] The internal discord between the rational decision to kill oneself and the irrational wish to live is well exemplified in Dostoevsky's portrayal of the last moments of Kirillov's life. Only when the will to live is totally subdued by the wish to die can one kill oneself without regrets or internal struggle.

It has been often said that man kills himself when the terror of death becomes less terrifying than the horror of life, that inclinations to suicide appear when the complete exhaustion of love of life sets in. Man is ready to kill himself when life loses its meaning to him, when all illusions are gone and when he is unable to bridge the gap between himself and his own life. According to Camus "judging whether life is or is not worth living amounts to answering the fundamental question of philosophy."[38] For Camus, "Dying voluntarily implies that you have recognized, even instinctively, the ridiculous character of that /life/ habit, the absence of any profound reason for living, the insane character of that daily agitation and the uselessness of suffering."[39] Logically life makes no sense in a world in which man is an outcast. But man is a stranger not only to others. There exists also a "divorce between man and his life, the actor and the setting,"[40] which Camus calls the feeling of absurdity. Absurdist reasoning, however, does not advocate self-destruction. The absurd man accepts reality. He is a man "who without negating it, does nothing for the eternal ... assured of his temporally limited freedom, of his revolt devoid of future and his mortal consciousness, he lives out his adventure within the span of his life time."[41] For the absurd man suicide would mean the end of the desperate encounter between human inquiry and the silence of the universe; absurdist reasoning considers that it could not consent to this without negating its own premises.[42]

It is clear that different people kill themselves for different reasons. Some take their lives from boredom, idleness, ennui or loneliness; for others suicide is an escape, an admission of personal bankruptcy and a sign of total alienation. There are as many different reasons for suicide to occur as there are suicides. In fact we can only speculate about the real motives which induce one to kill oneself. A successful suicide takes the secret into the infinite darkness of the grave. It is not given to man to experience death. When Levin, in Tolstoy's *Anna Karenina*, watches his dying brother, he has a feeling "of envy for the knowledge the dying man now possessed that was denied to him."[43]

Psychologists and psychoanalysts study the problem of suicide by compiling psychological autopsies of those who kill themselves. It is a process which involves obtaining pscyhological data about the behaviour and statements of a person deceased in the days prior to his death. But no psychological autopsy can reveal the real state of mind of a man at the very moment when he puts the gun to his head and pulls the trigger. The state of emotions and interrelation between the rational and irrational forces which determine ones actions in the last seconds of life cannot be established scientifically. Much of the data about the causes, motives and internal mechanisms of suicide is at best hypothetical. Imaginative literature therefore has a certain advantage over those who study the psychology of suicide, because a creative writer is not required to adhere too closely to scientific and scholarly conventions. He can depict the death of his protagonists in a manner he considers most fitting.

Suicide and Society

Whatever the reasons for suicide, whether one kills oneself for economic, personal or philosophical reasons, the act reflects, in a way, the conditions and trends prevailing in a given society. Man is always exposed to the judgement of the society of which he is a part. In the second half of the nineteenth century, Russian society continued to adhere, at least officially, to the values and the ethics propounded and advocated by the Russian Orthodox

Church. In fact, the attitude of the Russian Church to suicide was more inimical than that of other Christian denominations. In general terms "various faiths have taken every conceivable view of suicide, from recommending it to resolutely and uncompromisingly opposing it."[44] The early Christians followed the Platonic view of suicide. Both Plato and Aristotle "objected to self-destruction as cowardly and an offence against the state, which thus loses a citizen."[45] Beginning with St. Augustine, the Christian view of suicide becomes more unequivocal. St. Augustine establishes the sinfulness of every form of self-destruction by asserting "that suicide is an act which precludes the possibility of repentance and that it is a form of homicide, and therefore a violation of the sixth commandment."[46] The attitude of non-theological thinkers to the problem of self-destruction is more tolerant than that of dogmatic religious thought. It gravitates towards a compromise between the extreme view expressed by the representatives of the philosophical school of Stoicism which condones or even commends suicide on the one hand, and by the followers of the Kantian school who exhibit extreme rigidity in their approach to suicide and regard it as an insult to humanity, on the other.

In Tsarist Russia suicide cases were dealt with in ecclesiastical courts. When committed by a sane person in full control of his mental faculties, suicide was considered a grave sin. It was forbidden to bury those who killed themselves at a cemetery or near a church. The last will of the suicide was usually cancelled and he was refused Christian burial. According to the Army and Navy Regulations of Peter the Great, the body of a suicide was to be hanged by its legs or handed over to the executioner to be dragged away into a remote and disgraced place for burial. Soldiers and sailors attempting suicide could be sentenced to death. Those who were accused of attempting suicide were expected to repent and were punished at the discretion of the ecclesiastical authorities. An individual who induced or helped someone to commit suicide was regarded as an accomplice in murder and could be convicted to up to fifteen years of hard labour.[47]

Even though the Russian Church condemned suicide as sinful, it does not mean in the least that there were no suicides among the faithful. To the contrary, many members of different religious sects killed themselves in order to obtain blissful immortality or with the purpose of avoiding something which they regarded as polluting. Thus, for example, in Tiraspol, in 1897, twenty-eight persons buried themselves alive to escape the census which they apparently regarded as sinful. In 1666 many Russian zealots looked for the appearance of Antichrist. To escape him and to enter heaven, suicide was strongly urged by certain wrong-headed and often wholly criminal persons, clerical or lay.[48] It is well known that the rate of suicide among the Russian schismatics was much higher than among ordinary Orthodox people and that incidents of collective suicide among them have taken place on numerous occasions. According to one source in the second half of the seventeenth and eighteenth centuries, over ten thousand Russian schismatics died through self-immolation.[49].

It is apparent that the growth of the suicide rate in nineteenth century Russia is related to the growth of urbanization and industrialization. It is suggested by Thomas G. Masaryk that "the suicide tendency of the present rests upon the delusions of civilization."[50] "The primitive people show no suicide tendency at all; the civilized peoples, on the other hand, show a very intensive one."[51] In times of war, famine or social strife people seldom kill themselves. The instinct of self-preservation and the will to live then become the dominant factors motivating man's actions. Material well-being generates a thirst for spiritual fulfilment and a search for a meaning in life. Hungry people seldom kill themselves because they have an objective in life; they have to search for earthly bread to feed their families.

The hall-mark of the growth of nineteenth century civilization was the rapid development of the sciences, technological progress and the evolution of modern philosophical thought. Leading nineteenth century thinkers questioned the basic economic and social premises of contemporary society and challenged the religious ethics which are supposed to form the foundation of the existing social structure. The nineteenth century was one in which, more than at any other time, philosophical, ethical and religious values were questioned and re-evaluated. It was also a century in which a double sense of moral values became prevalent. It was a time in which true religiosity, which is based on faith in the irrational, was replaced by a superficial adherence to tradition and ritual. No wonder, therefore, that some thinkers associated the rapid growth of the nineteenth century suicide rate with irreligiosity, because both suicide and irreligiosity are the by-products of a rapidly developing civilization. Thus, for example, Masaryk could suggest that "in the final analysis the morbid suicide tendency of the present is caused by the irreligiosity of the masses. Moreover, since we know that the suicide tendency increased in recent times and is increasing, irreligiosity must also have increased and be increasing with it. But if the morbid tendency appears periodically, it appears as an external sign of the periodic irreligiosity of the people."[52] One may disagree with this uni-dimensional and somewhat simplistic explanation of the general causes of suicide, but since some of Dostoevsky's views pertaining to the reasons for suicide are strikingly similar to those expressed above they are worth mentioning.

The idea that lack of faith inevitably leads to murder is developed in Dostoevsky's novels consistently. It culminates in Ivan Karamazov's (*The Brothers Karamazov*) proposition that if there is no immortality — everything is permitted. But since suicide is also a form of murder, Ivan's above assertion applies to the murder of self as well as to the murder of others. K. Mochulsky suggests that "metaphysically the murderer and the suicide are blood brothers, both are victims of disbelief and accomplices of death."[53]

One should note that at the turn of the past century scholars and thinkers, such as Masaryk, did not as yet have the scientific, psychological and sociological tools which are presently available to contemporary scholars for a multi-dimensional study of a phenomenon as important as suicide, and thus they sought an explanation to the problem in values and notions traditional for their times. As opposed to Masaryk, however, Dostoevsky is not a scientist but rather an imaginative artist. He is not bound by the confines accepted in the social sciences for the study of suicide and can venture through his fiction into a deeper exploration of man as he finds himself in the process of destroying his own being.

II. SELF-DESTRUCTIVE ELEMENTS IN DOSTOEVSKY'S EARLY WORKS

1. PRE-SIBERIAN PERIOD

Suicide is a daily occurrence in the life of modern society. For Dostoevsky suicide is also a literary device which can reflect the writer's Weltanschauung and his artistic conception of the world. It is not requisite that the depiction of suicide in fiction be an exact reflection of reality. This depiction, however, has to be truthful to life and psychologically convincing. If it is not, the reader may suspect that suicide is applied as an artistic device with the sole purpose of removing a hero whose role has been played out and who retards the further flow of the narrative. Of course, one does not necessarily have to kill oneself in order to destroy oneself. Self-destruction can be mental, psychological or spiritual as well as physical. Logically, self-destruction makes little sense because it solutions are negative: it only destroys. Nevertheless, man often acts in a manner detrimental to his own well-being.

Dostoevsky's early prose explores the self-destructive nature of man. There is no depiction of successful suicides in Dostoevsky's early works but self-destructive, escapist tendencies permeate most of his early narratives. Many protagonists of the young Dostoevsky act in a manner contrary to simple logic. They aspire to heights which are beyond their reach and have ambitions which can never be satisfied. Consequently they are doomed to failure which can take the form of physical death, spiritual anguish or mental stagnation. Referring to the fates of Dostoevsky's early heroes, Victor Terras suggests that "what makes 'ugly tragedies' out of the lives of Devushkin, Prokharchin, Ordynov, and Efimov is that they take upon themselves — or are given by fate — a role for which they are not fit, a role in which they must inevitably fail."[1]

In his first novel, the epistolary narrative *Poor People*, Dostoevsky presents a succession of downtrodden characters who are crushed by poverty and humilation. The poor student Pokrovsky dies of consumption. The starving civil servant Gorshkov is absolved of a charge of embezzlement but dies of what seems to be unexpected overwhelming happiness. It is evident from the novel that poverty and social conditions are at the root of much evil in society. Yet Dostoevsky does not mean to conclude that material well-being can solve the personal plight of man or that it can provide a single social solution to all human problems. The fate of Gorshkov illustrates Dostoevsky's above proposition vividly. Gorshkov is vindicated. He is reinstated in his previous position. He regains his honour and security, yet he dies at a time when to begin a new life seems most appropriate.[2]

The fate of Makar Devushkin is a good example of self-destructive, irrational instincts at work. Devushkin, a poor clerk, is pathetic, funny and inferior in every possible way. His life is a constant struggle for existence and for the preservation of his personal dignity. What appears to be a fatherly attachment to his young friend Varvara makes his life more meaningful but it also strains Makar's material and spiritual capabilities to its limits. At first Makar submits to fate by recognizing his inferior social position and by accepting reality. He acknowledges that "all the world is built upon the system that each one of us shall have to yield precedence to some other one, as well as to enjoy a certain power of abusing his fellows."[3] Devushkin is undisturbed by the fact that he is at the very bottom of this social ladder and he has no one to abuse. He knows that it is his destiny and he tries to live with it as best he can. When Makar is faced with the inevitability of losing his beloved Varvara, it is then that his subtle mental equilibrium is destroyed. Makar's powerful lyrical outburst in his final letter makes it clear that he loves Varvara truly and passionately. At the same time it makes one realize that his love for Varvara is self-destructive.

Makar has created for himself a dream, an illusion, which makes his dreary life more meaningful. He raises himself above the level allotted to him by fate in reaching out for something beyond his immediate grasp. When his dream is destroyed, his fall is terrible. It appears that Devushkin's infatuation with Varvara makes him lose his awareness of reality. There is a strong feeling that Devushkin is carried by the flow of life without seeking to or being able, to change it. He has no real enemies who would like to undermine his situation, yet he finds himself slowly moving towards an abyss. In the abyss life still exists, but it is a life which is equal to spiritual death. It is a life which is out of control and where man moves with increasing speed to total ruination. Devushkin is aware of this process. He is struggling, but he is constantly moving closer to his tragic end. When the danger of losing Varvara becomes apparent Makar falls into despair and starts drinking heavily and habitually. Makar cannot revert to his old self. His love for Varvara has destroyed his previous conception of life, replacing it with a dream. When his dream is destroyed nothing is left but a painful vacuum and a need to escape reality. His alcoholism is a form of escapism as well as a means of spiritual suicide.

Ivan Petrovich Goliadkin, the main hero of *The Double* (*Dvoinik*, 1846) is another character who is destroyed by a combination of external pressures and internal strain. Like Devushkin, Goliadkin is a copying clerk; but unlike the destitute Devushkin who helps to support his friend Varvara, Goliadkin has no one to care for and is in possession of a considerable sum of money. Devushkin is a healthy, normal human being in contrast to Goliadkin, who is mentally ill. In the very beginning we are not made aware of the exact nature of Goliadkin's illness, but the tone of the narrative, which centres around his illness, is set in its opening chapter. It concludes with Goliadkin's visit to a medical practitioner.

Goliadkin is presented as a man of unstable character. He is moody, suspicious and fearful. He is an inferior person who refuses to recognize his position in society. To himself he is a powerful man. As soon as he encounters other people he loses his confidence. His desires are much greater than his powers to fulfil them. Goliadkin's main ambition is to gain the acceptance and admiration of his colleagues and superiors. He seeks their respect in different ways, including flattery and intrigue, but he is always unsuccessful in his endeavours. Goliadkin's failure to satisfy his aspirations drives him to despair. He tries to compensate for what is lacking in himself through the creation of his own double. But this attempt is futile because the double, known as Goliadkin junior, appears to have no objectively real identity, and exists in

Goliadkin's imagination only. Throughout the story with each of Goliadkin's attempts to become accepted in society which usually ends in public scandal and his humiliation, his state of health deteriorates as he slowly but steadily moves towards total mental disintegration. In the end he tries to appease his own double who finally defeats him.

Goliadkin's failure to come to terms with his own double, a creature endowed with all the positive qualities Goliadkin is lacking himself, is the result of all the humiliation he has endured in his life and of the subconscious awareness that he cannot succeed in his attempt to gain public acceptance. This subconscious awareness depresses Goliadkin's intention to dominate his double who ultimately treats his creator in the same humiliating manner everyone else does. The relationship between Goliadkin and his double could be regarded as a dependence between two levels of the subconscious: the deeper level, formed as the result of long lasting humiliating experiences, dominates the higher level or the double, recently formed by our hero's need to find a solution to his personal dilemma.

It might appear that objectively there is no reason for Goliadkin's mental disintegration. He does not have personal enemies nor is there any reason for him to feel economic insecurity. His physical health appears to be good and his appearance is acceptable. Yet, in his personality prevail destructive signs of extreme splitting of the ego. These signs lead first to the upset of his mental balance and the appearance of the double and finally to his total mental breakdown and insanity. The splitting of Goliadkin's ego is generated by the internal disparity between what Goliadkin believes himself to be and what he actually is, betweenm his self-image and objective reality. Dostoevsky seems to be arguing that man's elevated notions about himself, his exaggerated expectations from life and his inability to appreciate and accept reality are harmful and self-destructive, leading in the end to complete mental disintegration.

Semen Ivanovich Prokharchin, the main hero of the story "Mr. Prokharchin" (*Gospodin Prokharchin*, 1846), is also a lowly civil servant. Prokharchin is a miser who manages to scrape together and save enough money for a comfortable life. And yet he dies in poverty and misery. His avarice, which is generated by his internal sense of insecurity and a fear for the future, leads to the fear of losing what is supposed to form the foundation of his future security and ultimately to his self-destructive isolation. Prokharchin's predicament is a vicious circle: the money, which is supposed to give him security, creates new fears and self-destructive guilt feelings which, in turn, eventually lead to his ruin. Prokharchin does not die because he is poor, but because he is driven to destruction by his inherent sense of insecurity and his needless fear of poverty. Prokharchin never makes use of his money. When his landlady and her tenants discover his hidden treasures, they are surprised and puzzled.

At the centre of the plot of Dostoevsky's next story, "The Landlady" (*Khoziaika*, 1847), is the relationship among the strong and mysterious old Murin, the submissive, young and beautiful Katerina and the lonely recluse with a passion for science, Ordynov. Ordynov is a dreamer who isolates himself from the outside world by seeking solace in his studies. His solitude, however, does not make him happy: "He becomes afraid for his life, for his activity, and even for his future.... All of a sudden he realizes that he was lonely all his life; that no one ever loved him, nor could he love anyone."[4] A chance occurrence leads to his meeting and passionate infatuation with Katerina. She appears to love Ordynov, but at the same time she is in total submission to the powers of Murin. In order to be close to Katerina, Ordynov rents a room in Murin's lodgings. It is a self-destructive move fraught with dangerous consequences. The strong Murin attempts to shoot his weak adversary whose life is saved by a sudden epileptic fit which afflicts the old man. Ordynov faces defeat in his struggle for Katerina. The dreamer is not a man of action. His weakness is his undoing. He does not have the necessary strength to stab Murin when he is drunk. He drops the knife at the most decisive moment.

Murin understands Ordynov well. He tells him: "Give a weak man his freedom and he will bind it himself and return it to you. Freedom to a foolish heart is of no use! One cannot survive with such habits!"[5] Ordynov is not a fool but he is feeble, vulnerable and indecisive. His passion for Katerina is self-destructive and the loss of his love object leads to his mental breakdown. He loses interest in the world around him becoming highly unsociable and overcome by mysticism and morbid depression.

The psychological make-up of Ordynov's character and his inability to cope with the challenges which life poses, affect also the fate of Katerina. She is a captive of Murin, overcome by his mystical powers and by her own fears of eternal perdition. J. Frank suggests that Katerina "has reached the point where she has begun to enjoy and to savor her own sorrow and sense of irremedial sinfulness,"[6] becoming thus the first character "in which Dostoevsky focuses on the psychology of masochism and begins to explore the subtle and unhealthy 'enjoyment' that can be derived from self-laceration and self-punishment."[7] It is possible to agree with the assertion that masochistic tendencies are indeed character traits apparent in Katerina's personality, but it is also necessary to qualify this allegation. Her impulsive passionate response to Ordynov's love is an indication that she is still capable of genuine human emotions. Ordynov's defeat has driven Katerina even deeper into submission to the dark mystical powers of Murin. Ordynov could have been the saviour of Katerina. Instead, in destroying himself, Ordynov advances her ruin and impels her to seek satisfaction in total submission and self-immolation.

The main protagonist of the story "Polzunkov" (*Polzunkov*, 1848), Osip Mikhailych, is also a weak character who is torn apart by the internal struggle between the sense of his own worth and a deep-rooted feeling of insignificance. Although it is difficult for Polzunkov to accept his social position, he submits readily to external pressures and ridicule acting as a buffoon to the delight of all those with whom he comes in contact. Polzunkov "was the most honest and honourable man in this world. He had, however, one small weakness, namely, upon the demand of anyone he could good-naturedly and unselfishly act in a vile manner with the only purpose of pleasing his fellow man."[8] Polzunkov appears to be a man of good nature, but his inner goodness is the cause of his failure. His desire to please everyone, with no regard to the consequences, is self-destructive. People take advantage of him and abuse him, deepening his sense of inferiority and the realization of his own insignificance.

As the title of the story "A Weak Heart" (*Slaboe serdtse*, 1848) indicates, its main hero, the copying clerk Vasia Shumkov, is by no means a character able to cope with the realities of his daily existence. Objectively there are no reasons for Vasia's downfall; he is liked by his superiors and friends and is in love and engaged to Lizan'ka. He breaks down for what might seem an insignificant reason — his alleged inability to finish an assignment on time for his benevolent superior. In fact, Vasia's inherent guilt complex is the cause of his disintegration. He "feels guilty *before himself*, he feel thankless to his own fate. He is subdued and shaken by his own happiness of which he considers himself unworthy."[9] Vasia is oppressed and crushed by his own happiness. He could perhaps accept his personal bliss, but only if it would be part of universal welfare and prosperity. His friend Arkadii tells him "because you are happy you want everyone, absolutely everyone, to be happy at once. You are hurt and troubled to be alone in your happiness."[10] Vasia cannot enjoy his own felicity when there is so much suffering everywhere. His weak heart cannot cope with the rapid onslaught of his emotions. This weakness leads to his mental breakdown and total madness. There are no apparent external reasons for Vasia's destruction. He is ruined by his own success. The self-destructive impulses of his weak and submissive nature disarm him making it impossible for him to face reality, to confront the simple challenges of daily life.

Emel'ian Il'ich, the main protagonist of "An Honest Thief" (*Chestnyi vor*, 1848), is another character driven to destruction by his deep-rooted sense of guilt. Emel'ian, an inveterate alcoholic, steals a pair of breeches from his benefactor Astafii in order to be able to support his drinking habit. In the beginning he refuses categorically to take responsibility for his thievery and he leaves the house in an apparent expression of protest against Astafii's suspicions. But in the end, before his death, he returns home to confess to the theft and to express remorse for his deed.

The title of the story is a contradiction in terms. A thief cannot be honest. The very nature of his occupation is based on deceit, fraud and trickery. But Emel'ian is essentially an honest man; he is no habitual thief, rather he is driven to theft by his addiction to alcohol. As a morally superior character he commits an act which he himself cannot tolerate. His sense of guilt is intensified by the kindness of Astafii who does not castigate him and is ready to forgive. Emel'ian's guilty conscience torments him and finally it kills him. He is destroyed by the internal dichotomy of his nature.

The fate of Emel'ian manifests clearly that there can be a great disparity between what man is and what he does, and that in real life man's actions do not necessarily express the essence of man himself. When a sense of guilt afflicts a strong character, it can turn into a constructive force leading to his self-criticism and self-improvement. When a feeling of guilt besets a weak character, it can produce a destructive effect leading to self-castigation and self-punishment. A feeling of guilt leads to Vasia Shumkov's mental disintegration and his madness. In the case of Emel'ian the sense of guilt generated by the disparity between his culpable deed and the spiritual essence of his nature result in his total physical annihilation.

The nameless narrator of "White Nights" (*Belye nochi*, 1848) is a lonely dreamer. He is a shy introvert who fantasizes most of the time. In the eight years he spends in Petersburg he hardly makes a single acquaintance. His unexpected encounter with Nastenka gives his life, for the first time, some real meaning. There is a feeling that his love for Nastenka could turn his life from dream into reality. But the narrator is not a fighter. Not only does he give up Nastenka without a fight, but when her fiancé disappears without trace he tries to help her find him. Though he surrenders his beloved when the man she has chosen returns, his timid heart sinks and his hope for a new future is destroyed.

The dreamer is selfless. He appears to be happy for the sake of Nastenka. He seems satisfied with his lot. He thinks that "a minute of real bliss is surely enough for a man's whole life."[11] The narrator asks very little from life claiming to be satisfied with what fate gives him. Yet he is happy in appearance only. In reality when he loses Nastenka, he becomes more despondent than ever before. Everything that surrounds him assumes new depressing contours and dejects him. It is obvious that the narrator's encounter with Nastenka and his unselfish deeds have done little good for him. He returns to his underground more dispirited than ever before. He now understands that there exists another and better world which is unattainable, a reality for which he reached out but onto which he could not hold.

The narrator of "White Nights" is doomed to stagnation in his lonely world. His moral altruism is valued by Nastenka but it does not win her. The unselfish weak hero is destroyed by his own goodness. Selflessness is a positive spiritual force which can lift man up to new heights and serve as a forceful and worthy stimulus in man's quest for spiritual fulfilment. Unfortunately, positive characters rarely benefit from their own goodness. Many succumb to the forces of mediocrity and pettiness in society; others are taken advantage of by people with no scruples. It is disconcerting that an ethical power such as selflessness can turn into a negative force able to destroy those who by virtue of their moral superiority could serve as a positive example for man and society.

Egor Efimov, the tragic hero of the unfinished novel *Netochka Nezvanova* (1849), is another Dostoevskian protagonist destroyed by his inability to accept reality. Efimov is obsessed with the idea that he is one of the greatest violinists, if not in the whole world, then at least in Petersburg. He believes that "he is hurt and haunted by fate, and that because of different intrigues against him, he remains misunderstood and unknown."[12] Efimov's dream turns into a self-destructive mania. He takes to drink and blames everyone, in particular his wife, for his misfortune. Efimov's terrible awakening occurs at the performance of a world-famous violinist who arrives in Petersburg to give a concert. He is overwhelmed by the talent of the visitor and by the realization of his own inferiority. Suddenly his life's dream is destroyed and his life becomes meaningless. From a martyr on the altar of the arts he instantly turns into a rag, unable to face the terrible truth that he has wasted his own life and that he has tormented, without the slightest reason, those who are close to him.

The internal discord in the psychological and emotional composition of Efimov's character, and the dissonance between what he is and what he imagines himself to be, lead to his downfall. The collapse of his distorted notion about his artistic capabilities casues his madness and death: "He died because such a death was a necessity to him, the natural consequence of all his life. He had to die when everything that supported his life suddenly collapsed.... He died when his last hope disappeared.... The truth blinded him with its unbearable radiance, and what has been a lie was proved to be a lie, even to the man himself."[13]

But Efimov destroys not only himself. His predicament leads to the death of his wife and it has a shattering effect on the fate of his step-daughter, Netochka, who for a long time regards him as her real father. Upon his arrival in Petersburg Efimov marries a widow with a small child. She is madly in love with him and worships his talent, but Efimov abuses her and constantly complains that she is in the way of his greatness. Netochka is afraid for her mother, but she passionately loves her father. After Efimov drives his unfortunate wife to death, Netochka becomes obsessed with a feeling of guilt for her mother's fate.

Efimov does not perish because of social injustice. He is destroyed by a combination of different factors determined by the personal qualities of his character. His suffering wife is destroyed because she is dedicated and faithful to the man she loves. Love is a force which can elevate the individual above the mediocrity of everyday life. If love is abused, if it is aimed at the wrong person and does not meet with reciprocity, love can destroy man. Efimov's wife pays with her life for what might seem her love for the wrong man. She dies in terrible agony for the future fate of Netochka. It is even suggested by one critic that she commits suicide in despair,[14] a fact which stresses the destructive influence of Efimov on the fate of his wife as well as the self-destructive escapist tendencies prevalent in her character. Efimov's wife does not surrender easily. She meets life head on. She suffers and struggles but she is fighting a losing battle, and is defeated by the dark inexorable powers of fate.

Victor Terras suggests that there is a basic trait which can be abstracted from most works written by the young Dostoevsky, namely, "a preoccupation with the futility of human existence. It is not tragedy in the usual sense that wrecks the lives of Dostoevsky's unhappy heroes: not a stroke of fate, not a hostile society, not the evil plot of an enemy.... The motif of futility is a basic trait not only of the structure but also of the entire texture of these works."[15] I think that it would be necessary to qualify this statement by adding that Dostoevsky is preoccupied not with the futility of human existence in general, but with the futility of the existence of his weak heroes who are unable to cope with life. Their existence is futile because they are doomed to spiritual stagnation or physical destruction anyway. The destruction of these weak heroes is usually caused by a combination of social, ethical, and primarily psychological factors. It might appear to the uninitiated observer that in Dostoevsky's early works such as, for example, *Poor People* and *The Double*, the fate of the protagonists is first of all determined by social conditions. One might even suppose that poverty is at the root of Devushkin's ruin and that Goliadkin's plight is influenced by the social stratification existing in nineteenth century Russia. In fact, most heroes in Dostoevsky's pre-Siberian prose perish, not because they cannot master the external world, but rather because they cannot master themselves.

At the centre of most of Dostoevsky's early narratives are characters who are invariably doomed to failure by a peculiar combination of personal character traits in whcih destructive and self-destructive elements play a dominant role. In his early works Dostoevsky presents an array of dreamers, faint hearts, buffoons, masochists, loners and born losers. These characters are unable to come to terms with themselves. They succumb to the internal contradictions and weaknesses of their personalities, failing to adapt to the needs of their social environment. Dostoevsky's dreamer is frustrated because he reaches out for something he can never attain. The lonely recluse is cut off from contact with the outside world and tends to produce his own illusory realm which is destroyed as soon as he comes in touch with real life. The hero with a guilt complex punishes himself because of the disparity between his actions and his moral sense of values. The megalomaniac is destroyed because of his unrealistic notions of his own potentialities. All are victims of irrational self-destructive instincts over which they exercise no control and of which they are not aware. This slow, self-destructive process leads Devushkin to alcoholism, Ordynov to morbid depression and stagnation, Goliadkin and Vasia Shumkov to madness, and Prokharchin, Emel'ian, and Efimov to physical annihilation. In Dostoevsky's pre-Siberian fiction, the few strong characters who seem to be in control of their own destinies, such as Murin in "The Landlady" or Petr Aleksandrovich in *Netochka Nezvanova*, are negative, enigmatic and destructive.

Following in the steps of Gogol', the young Dostoevsky selects as his hero the lowly clerk, the downtrodden poor civil As opposed to Gogol' whose protagonist is submissive and humble and expects little from life, Dostoevsky's early hero reaches out for the impossible. Instead of attaining it, he faces inevitable doom. Self-destruction becomes a compositional device which demonstrates the futility of aspirations which cannot be fulfilled. Structurally, irrational self-destructive tendencies, prevalent in the natures of Dostoevsky's most important early heroes, move the development of the plots and lead the stories to conclusions which culminate in the ruin of their main characters.

The fate of the characters, appearing on the pages of Dostoevsky's early prose foreshadows, in a way, the themes which permeate Dostoevsky's major novels. In his first stories Dostoevsky already faces the reader with a number of monumental human problems to which man has no readily available solutions. He makes one aware of the fact that man is both rational and irrational, and that he often acts against his own logical interests. He induces his reader to believe that fate is unpredictable and that the notion of man being the master of his own destiny is a delusion. Dostoevsky makes the reader appreciate the great riddle of human nature: why one person has the inner capacity for happiness, while another is torn apart by anguish and internal contradictions; why one person is at peace with himself and with others, while his neighbour can neither accept his fellow man nor understand even himself.

2. POST-SIBERIAN PERIOD

Dostoevsky's immediate post-Siberian fiction reflects to a large extent his prison experience. His observation and close scrutiny of the criminal element in prison greatly influenced his understanding of human nature and made a lasting impact on his approach to human problems. The eight years Dostoevsky spent in Siberia also prompted a cardinal change in his Weltanschauung. E.H. Carr suggests that Dostoevsky learned in prison "to adjust himself to the abnormal world; and when he emerged his distorted vision was incapable of adjustment to any other focus. Normal men are as rare in Dostoevsky's novels as they must have been in the prison compound."[1]

Dostoevsky's pre-Siberian prose is dominated by weak characters who succumb to internal pressures and fall victim to the complexities of their own natures. At the centre of Dostoevsky's post-Siberian fiction usually are strong characters who dominate, and cause the destruction of, others. These strong domineering personalities are usually negative characters who use their destructive powers to suppress the positive impulses in those with whom they come in touch. In consequence the pressured hero destroys himself in an abrupt, often violent, manner as opposed to the pre-Siberian hero whose self-destruction is inexorable but slow and gradual.

A case in point is the fate of the teacher Vasia, from the story "Uncle's Dream" (*Diadiushkin son*, 1859), whose death is precipitated by an unsuccessful suicide attempt. At the centre of "Uncle's Dream" is the strong-willed Mar'ia Aleksandrovna Moskaleva. She is a shrewd and cunning woman who bullies everyone in sight. She attempts to control to social life in the town of Mordasov as well as the lives of her husband and daughter Zina. Zina is a proud and beautiful woman of twenty-three. She is loved and courted by the young official Pavel Mozgliakov, but her mother wants her to marry the old and wealthy Prince K. Zina herself, however, is in love with Vasia, a destitute teacher, the son of a sexton. Vasia, in the past a tutor to Zina's deceased brother, is a dreamer, an aspiring poet and an avid student of Shakespeare. Zina wants to marry him but they have a quarrel and she slaps him in the face. Vasia is furious. In order to avenge himself for the insult, he makes public Zina's secret love letter to him. The same evening, in what might seem as an act of remorse, he makes an unsuccessful attempt to poison himself.

Although the artistic conception of Vasia the dreamer is in Dostoevsky's pre-Siberian tradition, the outline of his character and the portrayal of his self-destructive endeavours have been influenced by Dostoevsky's prison experience. On his death bed Vasia tells Zina that his attempted suicide follows the example of a certain convict "who turned out to be a most cowardly man, when faced with punishment. Realizing that a sick man will not be punished he steeped snuff in wine and drank it. He was vomiting so long that he hurt his lungs. He was taken to hospital where he died several months later from consumption."[2] Vasia admits to Zina that he "decided to do away with himself in a similar manner"[3] because he wanted to die a slow death instead of killing himself instantaneously. He is motivated by a sweet romantic notion that when Zina finally realizes that she is the cause of his forthcoming death she will suffer terribly and beg his forgiveness.

It is obvious that Vasia's attempted suicide and death have been inspired by Dostoevsky's own predicament in Siberia. The convict in whose steps Vasia follows is reminiscent of one of the criminals depicted by Dostoevsky in the *House of the Dead* (*Zapiski iz mertvogo doma*, 1860-62) who will do anything to avoid or even postpone impending flogging. M.S. Al'tman points out correctly that Vasia is modelled after the convict Ustiantsev[4] whom the narrator of the *House of the Dead* encountered in the prison hospital. We are told that the narrator

> "knew a convict, a young man who had been a soldier, condemned for murder to the maximum number of strokes. He was so panic-stricken that on the eve of the punishment he drank off a jug of vodka in which he had previously soaked snuff.... The poor fellow after drinking his jug of vodka was at once taken ill in earnest; he began vomiting blood and he was carried to the hospital almost unconscious. The vomiting so affected his chest that in a few days he showed unmistakable signs of consumption, of which he died six months later."[5]

Vasia's fate is similar to that of Ustiantsev. His initial suicide attempt is unsuccessful but he comes down with consumption and dies soon after. Vasia's dream has been partially realized. Zina spends the last minutes of his life at his bed-side, but his self-destruction serves no useful purpose. Upon seeing the dead body of her son Vasia's mother curses Zina, but this does not prevent Zina from making a good match by marrying an elderly Governor-General in a remote province.

Vasia's death is the first attempt at physical suicide in the works of Dostoevsky. The young teacher hurts himself because he wants to evoke the sympathy of the woman he loves but he also wants to punish her at the same time by making her feel guilty for his suffering. Deep in his heart Vasia hopes that the poison will not kill him, that he will be spared the fate of the dead convict. Ustiantsev's attempted suicide is a cowardly act undertaken with the purpose of escaping physical pain. Vasia's act is a cowardly reaction to an unfulfilled love; it is an act of despair doomed to failure.

Although Vasia is in many ways similar to Dostoevsky's pre-Siberian romantic dreamers, the author does not idealize him. K. Mochulsky suggests that

> "in the 'Uncle's Dream' the romantic *dreamer is entirely deposed.* How dissimilar do we find the poet Vasya, an 'evil and shallow man,' to the dreamer Ordynov in the 'Landlady' or to the hero of 'White Nights'! The author judged his youth sternly; that by which he used earlier to live was now 'sweet romantic nonsense.' The dreamer, torn away from life, was simply a '*worthless individual.*' And so after his political repentance began his exposure of literary idols. Romanticism was condemned as moral corruption."[6]

In the predicament of Vasia Dostoevsky discards his old notion of the self-destructive romantic dreamer. "Uncle's Dream" foreshadows the creation of an array of new heroes who act violently, often on impulse, destroying themselves for a variety of internal and external reasons.

Vasia's deed is the only example of intended violent self-destruction in Dostoevsky's works prior to *Crime and Punishment.* In his other early, post-Siberian works following the "Uncle's Dream," destruction is forced upon the weak and positive characters by strong negative heroes. The confrontationm between the strong destructive protagonists and the positive elements embodied in the upright characters expresses the ongoing struggle between good and evil in human nature and society.

Foma Fomich Opiskin, one of the main protagonists of *The Village of*

Stepanchikovo and Its Inhabitants (*Selo Stepanchikovo i ego obitateli*, 1859), is an example of such a negative destructive character who attempts to dominate, bully, and drive into submission all those around him. Foma Fomich is a vain, voluptuous braggart and jester. He is a discontented man of letters whose morbid passion for self-exaltation knows no limits. He is a despot, an hypocrite who takes pleasure in tormenting and humiliating his benefactor, the weak but amiable colonel Egor Il'ich Rostanev. The colonel submits to Foma's tyranny and his own destructive pressures but when Foma maligns Nasten'ka, the governess of his children and the woman he loves, Egot Il'ich comes to her defence and rebels against Foma.

In general, the colonel's selfless nature succumbs to the ruinous powers of Foma. Although he cannot defend himself from Foma, he reacts violently on behalf of those who are most in need. Unexpectedly he ejects Foma from the house, after which the latter soon returns confused and allegedly reformed, to exercise on the household as powerful an influence for good as he had previously exercised for evil. One can, of course, doubt Foma's transformation and the sincerity of his actions. N. Chirkov suggests that the "boundaries between Foma's sincerity and his conscious acting, between his sincerity and hypocrisy seem to disappear, but actually remain untouched."[7] It is possible only to suspect that the destructive instincts of Foma's character have not disappeared overnight. His cowardly nature adapts itself to the changing circumstances of his life but his internal destructive powers could come again to the fore when the time becomes more opportune.

Prince Petr Aleksandrovich Valkovsky, the enigmatic hero of *The Insulted and Injured* (*Unizhennye i oskorblennye*, 1861), is another embodiment of evil who affects negatively, and drives to destruction, a number of characters who are essentially good people. Valkovsky is a two-faced sensualist and a man without principles. He recognizes nothing that does not bring personal advantage or pleasure. He stops at nothing in order to achieve his objectives. His life path is strewn with victims, both physically destroyed or spiritually and emotionally ruined. Valkovsky drives to death his two wives, the mothers of Alesha and Nelly respectively, as well as Nelly and her grandfather, the old Smith who died destitute. He shatters the life of young Natasha Ikhmenev, also humiliating her parents and destroying their future.

As the title of the novel suggests, the plot centres around the fate of the insulted and the injured — people who submit to the dark forces of destiny which manifest themselves in the destructive scheming of Valkovsky. His ruinous designs, however, are facilitated by the pscyhological make up and the actions of his victims who fail to perceive his cunning nature. Natasha falls in love with Valkovsky's son Alesha, a simple-hearted and naive young man, who abandons her for a wealthy bride selected for him by his deceitful father. The old Ikhmenevs, Natasha's parents, are ruined by coming to Petersburg in order to seek justice from Valkovsky without realizing that they are no match for this sly manipulator. Nelly's mother dies in poverty because she falls in love with Valkovsky, a man who cheats her out of her money and abandons her with child on hand. Nelly is downtrodden and dies in agony because, like her mother, she accepts suffering rather than seeking justice from her perfidious father.

The acceptance of material and physical suffering can lead to fatal consequences and destroy man's life but, as it is shown in Dostoevsky's major novels, it can also enlighten man and lead to his spiritual fulfilment. In this respect self-sacrifice and suffering could be regarded as positive factors in the life of man as he moves towards spiritual illumination and regeneration. However, in *The Insulted and Injured* the suffering of many heroes leads to their total bodily annihilation, leaving no room for a spiritually enlightened life.

Valkovsky embodies many traits characteristic of the convicts depicted in *The House of the Dead.* Most of them have an insatiable thirst for life and for freedom. A prisoner's actions are calculated to his immediate advantage and are aimed at improving his chances for survival. Most prisoners not only are in conflict with the social law, but also place themselves beyond the accepted confines of the moral law. They are determined people and they usually have strong personalities.

The title of the book *House of the Dead* is paradoxical. It might appear from the title that the inhabitants of this house are dead in body or in spirit, that most of them succumb to the pressures of a difficult life and give reign to their self-destructive instincts. In fact the opposite is true. The prisoner's craving for life is almost impossible to satisfy — physical survival becomes his sole pre-occupation.

> "Every convict feels that he is, so to speak, *not at home* but on a visit. He looks at twenty years as though they were two, and is fully convinced that when he leaves prison at fifty-five he will be as full of life and energy as he is now at thirty-five."[8]

Many criminals exhibit self-destructive, even suicidal tendencies prior to their conviction, but once in prison the longing for freedom becomes the convict's prime objective in life. Thus, for example, unable to cope with the difficult life of a recruit, the young Sirotkin tries to shoot himself. When this attempt fails he sticks a bayonet into his officer, earning himself a life sentence in prison.[9] Sirotkin's self-destructive instinct turns into a destructive force because both tendencies are prompted by the same motive: the desire, at any price, to escape an intolerable life situation with no regard to future consequences.

Akim Akimych, one of the few upper class Russians in prison, is a phenomenally honest man. In the past a lieutenant in command of a fortress in the Caucasus, he takes justice into his own hands by ordering an allied chieftain shot for burning his fortress while making a perfidious night assault upon it. Akim Akimych at once sends in a full report of this incident to the authorities. In consequence he is sentenced to penal servitude in Siberia for twelve years.[10] Akim Akimych knows that according to the law what he did was wrong, but he feels that according to his own sense of justice he was right. He knows that he performed a deed for which he will be severely punished. Akim Akimych is no coward; he ruins his future and chooses a life of misery and physical privation because he is faithful to his principles and is ready to suffer for them.

It is paradoxical that while *House of the Dead* deals with a most depressing environment in which crime, torture and tragedy are daily reality, it is at the same time one of Dostoevsky's most optimistic works. It is optimistic because most characters have a strong craving for life.

For Dostoevsky, suffering and privation do not kill man nor do they drive him to suicide. Difficult life generates a desire for a better life and, therefore, for life in general. Dostoevsky's prisoners have no need to search for the meaning in life; their objective in life is physical survival and freedom and they fervently hope that they can attain it. Hope is the single most important factor that moves man out of self-destructive and suicidal preoccupation. As soon as there is no hope for a better future, life becomes aimless. A good example, in this respect, is the narrator of the *House of the Dead*, Aleksandr Petrovich Gorianchikov. He survives ten years of penal servitude in Siberia, but he dies soon after having been set free. The thirst for freedom and the desire to survive give his life in prison significance but once outside the prison walls his lonely life becomes aimless and he dies in solitude at the young age of thirty-five.

According to R.L. Jackson, "*House of the Dead* constitutes the great divide in Dostoevsky's works. It profoundly influenced every work that followed."[11] Jackson argues that "in its themes and preoccupations *House of the Dead* anticipates the problem content of Dostoevsky's novels in the 1860s and 1870s."[12] The *House of the Dead* is central to Dostoevsky's future artistic output because his Siberian experience is at the root of the transformation of his Weltanschauung, and because it has greatly influenced the evolution of his creative method. Life in prison gave also Dostoevsky an excellent opportunity to observe the ways of the Russain peasant and to study the psychology of violence and criminal behaviour.

The destructive violence exhibited by the criminal in Siberia is in most cases an expression of his instinct for self-preservation. The violence displayed by Dostoevsky's post-Siberian characters is both destructive and self-destructive but at the same time it expresses man's strong attachment to life. Since Dostoevsky's post-Siberian art concentrates mainly on the extreme manifestations of human nature, it abounds in many acts of violence, including suicide. This final act of self-destruction becomes possible because most of Dostoevsky's later heroes are decisive and bold individuals, people who resemble closely the criminals encountered by Dostoevsky in Siberia. Thus, the weak "faint hearted" dreamer, depicted in the pages of Dostoevsky's early prose, is replaced by a strong and determined character. The devastating latent self-destructive tendencies which lead to the ruin of his early heroes are thus transformed in his mature fiction into violent acts of self-destruction, the murder of self.

III. MAJOR WORKS OF FICTION

It has become customary to consider the "Notes from Underground" (*Zapiski iz podpol'ia*, 1864) as an introduction and philosophical preface to Dostoevsky's major novels. The "Notes", which are the confession of a nameless narrator, underscore the notion that man is an irrational creature, and therefore reason alone cannot explain the intricate nature of man.

In the first part of the narrative the underground man expounds the theoretical premises of his philosophy; in the second part his philosophy is tested in action. The underground man relates here a number of incidents from his life which illustrate clearly that man often acts against his own best interests by provoking abuse, humiliation and pain, which can lead to extreme physical or emotional suffering. In fact the whole book is a logical argument for one's right to harm oneself by acting in a manner contrary to one's own rational advantage and benefit.

The underground man is a spiteful, miserable, petty tyrant with a craving for dominance. His isolation is supported by his brilliant reasoning which finds justification for his solitude. His brilliance of thinking depends on his isolation. He finds that he is able to judge others because he is more lucid when not involved with them. He is a thinker and a dreamer who, when removed from the world, is capable of inventing feelings, even of love, out of sheer boredom. It is this perpetual consciousness, however, which makes it impossible for him to experience any true human emotions.

The underground man is a sick man, but he refuses to see a doctor. He could be in severe physical pain but he will suffer rather than resort to outside help. He develops a philosophy which justifies the need for, and pleasure of, suffering. His suffering is not the kind which leads to spiritual illumination, rather it is a suffering which makes him aware of his physical being and his unlimited freedom. The underground man does nothing for his own well-being. Instead, he advocates both physical and spiritual self-destruction, while exhibiting at the same time an irrational craving for life. His mental isolation and spiritual stagnation are his solitude. He creates a physical underground and this state generates the question: is physical life at all worthwhile or necessary. Without a twinge of conscience he preaches his own doom by saying that he is "forty now, and forty years is a whole life — forty is deep old age. It's indecent, vulgar, and immoral to live beyond forty!"[1]

The underground man despises the spontaneous man of action. He considers him limited and stupid, because he mistakes the nearest secondary causes for primary ones. He contrasts the man of action with the man of heightened consciousness who will not act unless he knows the primary cause. The hyperconscious man knows that there is no rational way of learning about the essence of the primary cause, and therefore he does not act but retreats into his underground. According to the underground man, the man of action looks for a meaning in life, in the rational organization of society, which should be advantageous and useful to him, without realizing that he himself remains irrational and contradictory. As an hypersensitive individual, the underground man can find no satisfaction in rational social organization and, therefore, his life is meaningless.

In the first original version of "Notes from Underground" Dostoevsky alludes to the notion that meaning in life should be sought in faith in Christ, a remark removed unceremoniously by the censors. In a letter to his brother Michael, Dostoevsky complains that the misprints in the "Notes" are terrible and that

> "It would have been better not to print the next to last chapter at all (the most important one, where the essential thought is expressed), than to print it as it is, i.e., with sentences torn out and full of contradictions. But what can be done! Those swine of censors — the passages where I mocked everything and sometimes *made show* of blaspheming are allowed, but the passages where I deduced from all this the need of faith and Christ — that is suppressed."[2]

It appears that, according to Dostoevsky, the rational purpose of human existence, which man seeks by identifying with a social structure which upholds his interests and gives him an illusory feeling of having an objective in life, should be replaced by faith in Christ which is the only force able to make life truly meaningful. Without faith life is aimless and meaningless; and, therefore, lonely and self-destructive, often leading to spiritual stagnation and even to total physical annihilation. But the reasoning of the hyperconscious underground man leads to a paradoxical predicament. He argues in his monologue for the irrational essence of man. He exerts all his mental capabilities to prove that the rational organization of society, which fails to recognize the irrational nature of man, leads the individual into a dead end. But, the underground man refuses to accept anything on trust, including the non-rational theory of religion. He rejects faith in the irrational and he demands for himself absolute freedom, a freedom which negates all that man stands for. To Dostoevsky genuine freedom is freedom in Christ, the freedom of affirmation which is not the acceptance of social rules, but rather an affirmation of an innate positive and sympathetic feeling of one human being for another.

According to an idea expressed by Dostoevsky in his "Winter Notes on Summer Impressions" (*Zimnie zametki o letnikh vpechatleniiakh*, 1863), self-sacrifice and an individual's altrusitic identification with his fellow man is the highest form of expression of a fully developed personality: "Voluntary, totally conscious, and unforced self-sacrifice for the benefit of all, is ... a sign of the highest development of personality, of its greatest power, its greatest self-control, the highest expression of the freedom of its own will. To sacrifice one's life voluntarily for others, to be crucified, burned at the stake for all, is possible only when one's individuality is most fully developed."[3]

The underground man cannot sacrifice himself for others, nor can he accept irrational faith. Instead, he is enslaved by his ideas of absolute freedom, by his inner contradictions and by the dual essence of his nature. Rationally, he advocates the irrational; but he himself refuses to accept what he preaches to others. This dilemma is the cause of his solitude and loneliness. It drives him into his self-destructive underground which contributes to his spiritual disintegration.

According to Horney's theory of suicide

> "a sudden impulse of self-hatred in a framework of severe alienation may initiate suicidal behaviour.... A slow form of suicide occurs when the idealized self invests the self with ugliness and slothfulness,

> degrading the self.... Another form of self-destruction occurs when the person 'silently but actively collaborates towards his own moral deterioration.' This also is based on alienation, with the person cynically opposed to integrity, which he considers a form of weakness."[4]

There is no question that the theories and actions of the underground man conform neatly with Horney's theory of suicide. It is quite logical, therefore, to suggest not only that the underground man commits spiritual suicide but also that he has great potential for total physical self-destruction.

More than a decade after the publication of "Notes from Underground" Dostoevsky develops further the ideas expressed in the original, unexpurgated version of the "Notes" by stating bluntly in *The Diary of a Writer* (*Dnevnik pisatelia*, 1873-81) that only materialists and atheists who have no faith in God or immortality usually commit suicide.[5] The predicament of the underground man foreshadows, in a sense, the tragic destinies of Dostoevsky's future fictional thinkers and intellectuals, such as, for example, Raskolnikov (*Crime and Punishment*), Stavrogin, or Ivan Karamazov who lose their inner peace and destroy their future happiness. They wage a struggle with God and in the end refuse to accept anything beyond their immediate rational grasp.

The rational deliberations of the underground man, which are to substantiate his theory of the irrational essence of human nature, lead to his spiritual suicide. Similarly, the behaviour and actions of Aleksei Ivanovich, the narrator of *The Gambler* (*Igrok*, 1866), who succumbs to the overpowering irrational passion for gambling, lead to his spiritual, emotional and mental disintegration. The predicament of Aleksei Ivanovich illustrates clearly the inability of man to control his irrational impulses. The gambler is drawn to the gaming tables neither by greed nor by a thirst for material gain. He is well aware that should he win a substantial amount of money he will squander or lose it in no time. Instead, he is intoxicated by the insatiable thirst for special emotions. He is obsessed with the desire to take risks. His passion is his undoing for this irresistible power cannot be quenched or satisfied.

An addicted gambler becomes the passive tool of a dark force which little by little destroys his mind and his heart, leading eventually to his physical degeneration. Aleksei Ivanovich understands his situation. He is aware of his degradation and utter helplessness. He asks himself: "What am I? I am zero — nothing. What shall I be tomorrow? I may be risen from the dead, and have begun life anew. For still I may discover the man in myself, if only my manhood has not become utterly shattered."[6] Unfortunately, the gambler's rational hope for a better future is based on his confidence that he still can win at the roulette table. It is a delusion fraught with terrible consequences. Instead of being saved by keeping away from the gaming tables, the gambler seeks a solution to his dilemma by returning to the very source of his tribulations. The gambler destroys himself step by step, giving in to his irresistible, irrational craving for unique sensations.

The life styles of both the underground man and Aleksei Ivanovich, are influenced by the self-destructive inclinations prevailing in their natures. The underground man is a brilliant thinker whose self-destruction seems to be rational and premeditated. He appears to be in control of his mental faculties and his ruin is an expression of his freedom of choice. The ruin of the narrator of *The Gambler*, on the other hand, is the result of his inability to control his emotions. He is doomed because he cannot overcome the irrational disparity between his rational mind and his irrational passion.

Self-destructive and destructive elements are dominant character traits in Dostoevsky's early prose. These traits often influence the development of the plots determining the evolution of the fates of many protagonists. By embarking upon the study of the psychology of self-destructive behaviour in man, Dostoevsky becomes one of the predecessors of the psychologists and psychoanalysts of the twentieth century. According to S. Freud, "there exist from the beginning in all of us strong propensities toward self-destruction and these come to fruition as actual suicide only in exceptional cases in which many circumstances and factors combine to make it possible."[7] To Freud, "the manifestations of the self-destructive instinct were never nakedly visible."[8]

In Dostoevsky's early works dormant self-destructive propensities drive his heroes slowly but surely to total ruin, in the form of spiritual, emotional, mental or physical destruction. In his novels these propensities come to fruition in the violent suicide of those concerned. Thus, the circle closes. The dramatic construction, the tragic conception and the philosophical significance of Dostoevsky's major novels require a new approach to problems of self-destruction in which hidden, slowly-acting, self-destructive behaviour is replaced by forceful, rapid, impetuous acts of suicide. In certain instances physical and spiritual corruption and self-destruction can lead, in Dostoevsky's novels, to physical degeneration and suffering which are followed by spiritual regeneration, while, at other times, physical and spiritual disintegration lead to total physical annihilation by the violent murder of self.

1. CRIME AND PUNISHMENT (PRESTUPLENIE I NAKAZANIE, 1866)

Raskolnikov

There are a number of committed, attempted and contemplated suicides in *Crime and Punishment.* Most important for the structure and the meaning of the novel are Raskolnikov's contemplated self-destruction and the actual suicide of Svidrigailov. Although the other suicides appear to be of secondary importance, they are in fact of great significance in the composition of the plot. The fates of these minor heroes are closely linked to the destinies of the major characters in the novel. Their actions shed light on the nature and human qualities of the main protagonists and even foreshadow their actions.

The general theme of physical self-destruction and the idea of Raskolnikov committing suicide occupied the author's mind from the very early stages of his work on the novel. There are many references in Dostoevsky's notebooks for the novel pertaining to Raskolnikov putting a bullet through his head.[1] In the final version of the novel, the idea of Raskolnikov shooting himself alternates with the notion of his taking his life by drowning himself in the Neva river. In addition, the idea of Raskolnikov's self-destruction alternates with his defiance of society and his strong will to live. On one occasion, in a state of mental instability, Raskolnikov walks in the Haymarket and engages in conversation there with some women of ill-repute. He ponders their fate as well as the value of life in general. He compares himself to a man condemned to die who "thought, that if he had to live on some high crag, on a ledge so small that there was no more than room for his two feet, with all about him the abyss, the ocean, eternal night, eternal solitude, eternal storm,... it would be better to live so, than die within the hour? Only to live, to live! No matter how — only to live!"[2]

The irrational impulse of self-destruction does not leave Raskolnikov in peace; it exists side by side with his fervent love for life. A while later, upon entering a tavern, Raskolnikov meets the police clerk Zametov, and challenges fate by alluding to his own association with the murder of the two women. Somewhat later, when Raskolnikov stands on the Voznesenskii Bridge, peering attentively into the waters of the canal, he witnesses a woman, Afrosiniushka, fling herself recklessly into the canal. The drowning woman is pulled out. She is saved and she quickly recovers, but the sight of the attempted suicide makes Raskolnikov consider his own predicament. He is repelled by the idea of meeting his end in the deep waters of the canal, yet he thinks that it is one of the few remaining paths he can follow.[3]

Although Raskolnikov appears to have no pangs of conscience for his crime on the rational level, subconsciously he is profoundly guilt-ridden. The image of the two murdered women pursues him relentlessly. According to psychoanalysts Karl Menninger a part of man's "conscience is unconscious; there are some things about which we feel guilty without knowing it."[4] And A.L. Bem suggests that the case of Raskolnikov is an extraordinary one because "despite the absence of an externally realized feeling of guilt, it does not only exist on the subsconsious level, but it also determines the final outcome of the human drama."[5] This subconscious feeling of guilt is also expressed in Raskolnikov's eagerness to challenge fate and to seek punishment. He goes to the scene of the murder, Alena's flat. He knows that it is dangerous, yet he craves to relieve his inner tension which is caused by the terrible spiritual blow and by the immediate effect of the crime upon his soul.

The attempted suicide of Afrosiniushka, witnessed by Raskolnikov, brings our hero to the verge of suicide. He is drawn time and again to the bridge, to the very place where Afrosiniushka jumped into the deep waters. And Raskolnikov faces the challenge. Afrosiniushka's rescue is mirrored by Raskolnikov's newfound strength to overcome the temptation of self-destruction within himself. He muses "my life did not die with the old woman.... Now comes the reign of reason and light ... and freedom and power ... now we shall see! Now we shall measure our strength! he added arrogantly, as though he were addressing some dark power and summoning it up."[6]

Is Raskolnikov really as strong as he claims to be, or is he just blinded by pride? On the one hand, Raskolnikov has to be strong and decisive to dare to overstep the law, to commit a crime and despite all inner confusion after the crime to still be able to assert the righteousness of his deed. On the other hand, Raskolnikov begins gradually to lose control of his rational faculties as he becomes increasingly obsessed with his fixed criminal idea. His subconscious takes the upper hand over his reasoning and he becomes progressively weaker.

Janko Lavrin considers Raskolnikov "a weak man crushed by a strong idea."[7] J. Middleton Murry claims that "Raskolnikov was for Dostoevsky, as he was for himself, merely the victim of his unsuccess and of his weakness."[8] Similarly, Nicholas Berdiaev asserts that "the tortured conscience of Raskolnikov is a witness not only to his transgression but also to his weakness."[9] N. Strakhov, on the other hand, considers Raskolnikov a strong character. He claims that Dostoevsky "clearly wants to represent a strong soul, a man full of life, not one who is demented and weak."[10] It seems difficult to classify Raskolnikov as either weak or strong. He is certainly not an ordinary character. He is introduced to us in a state of mental tension, of constant inner struggle which is usually beyond his control. He is a man with a very complex personality who in certain instances may appear to us as very strong, while at other times as utterly weak.

To the question of whether one has to be strong or weak in order to be able to take one's own life there is certainly no single answer. A weak-willed man often has difficulty in coping with his own existence because he is unable to change himself or the external conditions of his life. Suicide for such a man is an escape from an intolerable reality which is too difficult for him to master. A weak individual, however, is usually indecisive and may lack the inner strength and resolve necessary to take his own life. In contrast, a strong character may have the will power to destroy himself, but by the same token should also possess the power to fight and eliminate the causes leading to his suicide, i.e., to fight for a better life. An obvious paradox is apparent here, and, therefore, it is necessary to conclude that those committing suicide could be both strong and weak, the more so since there are no two people driven to suicide by the same reason.

In many actual and attempted suicides depicted by Dostoevsky, in particular those which are the result of rational and logical deliberations, as in the cases of Ippolit and Kirillov, the strength of will of those concerned is of utmost importance for the successful consummation of the intended self-destructive act. Yet even in such instances the actual act of self-destruction is in most cases rash, impulsive, even irrational. As for Raskolnikov, he cannot be classified with Ippolit or Kirillov in this respect because his rebellion is neither against God nor nature, but rather against social injustice, something he thinks is within his power to change. Ippolit and Kirillov decide to kill themselves in defiance of an order of things which is beyond their control. Raskolnikov, on the other hand, decides to murder someone else in his endeavour to singlehandedly improve the social and ethical composition of the society of which he is a part.

And yet, the idea of suicide haunts Raskolnikov until his very confession, and even after it. He views it not only aa a means of escaping punishment, but also as a way of fleeing shame and hateful reality. He applies this solution to all who seem to be in trouble. For example, upon learning from Sonia Marmeladov about the terrible fate of her family; about her own lofty character and the shameful means with which she is forced to support her stepmother and children, Raskolnikov readily suggests suicide to her. He says: "surely it would be better, a thousand times better and wiser, to plunger into the water and end it all."[11]

Even after having been condemned to penal servitude in Siberia, Raskolnikov cannot forgive himself for the weakness which prevented him from being able to take his own life. His misery and suffering are intensified because he has no answer to the question: "Why had he not killed himself? Why, when he stood on the bank of the river, had he chosen rather to confess? Was there really such strength in the will to live, and was it so difficult to overcome? Had not Svidrigaylov, who feared death, overcome it?[12]

The prosecuting magistrate, Porfiry Petrovich, is aware of Raskolnikov's hidden intentions to take his own life, but he considers him incapable of such a resolute step. At one of their meetings he tells Raskolnikov that "if anything happened (not that I think it will and I consider you quite incapable of it), if, by any chance — well just in case — you should feel a desire during the next forty or fifty hours to put an end to the matter differently, in some fantastic way — by raising your hand against yourself (a ridiculous supposition, you must please forgive me for it) then — leave a short circumstantial note."[13] At his last meeting with his sister Dunia, Raskolnikov confesses to her that he has to arrive at a decision as to how he will act and what he will do with himself. The only possible choice is surrender or suicide.

Raskolnikov has been strong enough to dare overstep the natural boundaries of human ethics and kill two innocent women, but he cannot privately sustain the moral responsibility for his crime. A human being with an innate positive balance between good and evil in his character can commit an act of conditional altruism, that is, a crime for the purpose of good, but after the crime he often undergoes a terrible punishment on the part of his conscience. Raskolnikov tells Dunia, "I wanted to reach a definite decision and I found myself walking near the Neva many times; I do remember that. I should have liked to end things there, but ... I decided against it.... And it was to escape the shame that I wanted to drown myself, Dunya, but the thought came to me, when I was already standing on the bank, that if I had hitherto considered myself strong, then the shame should not frighten me now."[14] But Raskolnikov's inner doubts and vacillations continue and we are never sure what he is going to do with himself next. When Sonia loses sight of him for a while she is "torturing herself with the fear that he might really commit suicide. Dunya felt the same fear."[15]

In the early drafts of the novel we read: "The end of the novel. Raskolnikov goes to shoot himself. Svidrigailov: I would go to America even now, but somehow no one wants to go. Svidrigailov tells Raskolnikov at the Haymarket, you shoot yourself and I will, perhaps, shoot myself." A few lines later Svidrigailov reiterates "shoot yourself, it is not with your character to remain alive. You have two paths: to confess or to shoot yourself."[16] In the final version of the novel Raskolnikov survives while Svidrigailov indeed shoots himself.

Why does Raskolnikov not kill himself? Why should we believe, what K. Mochulsky calls, Dostoevsky's "pious lie" about Raskolnikov's regeneration?[17] The answer to this question is provided by the very nature of Raskolnikov's innate human qualities and by the composition of the plot which requires a different solution to the personal drama of the main hero. Raskolnikov is a rational hero who oversteps his natural connection with the soil, but he is a man who has enough positive features within himself to make his return to the soil possible. The soil should not be viewed here in a narrow sense. It encompasses not only mother earth but also his real mother whom he loves dearly, as well as society at large for the sake of which, at least partially, he commits the crime. It is paraoxical that while Raskolnikov's theories appear to him socially significant and positive, and the murder is committed in part on behalf of society, the crime isolates him from the people with whom he appears to be concerned. Raskolnikov might be driven to his actions by social concerns but he underestimates the impact which the unwritten but universally accepted laws of human ethics can exert on a man's conscience.

In addition, one should not underestimate the role of Sonia Marmeladov as a catalyst, helping Raskolnikov's "return to life." Her deep faith and selfless compassion, her readiness both to help those in need and to suffer for the sins of others, are in striking contrast to the self-centred and rebellious character of Raskolnikov. Sonia's humble nature is able to exert a positive influence on Raskolnikov and help him emerge victorious in his inner struggle with the dark forces driving him to physical self-destruction.

V.Ia. Kirpotin suggests that "Raskolnikov lives not for death but for life, even more so for an idea, i.e., for life in general. Raskolnikov will not kill himself because he knows: death stops all relationships between existence and generations.... Raskolnikov does not consider death as a final solution, precisely because other people and their problems remain — life goes on."[18] It is possible to question whether social altruism, as Kirpotin suggests, is the single most important impulse which spares Raskolnikov from suicide. It is probably his inner craving for life and his desire to survive at any price that save our hero from self-destruction. It is a thirst for life which is characteristic of Dostoevsky himself. N. Strakhov suggests that Raskolnikov is "a man who very much wants to live, who quickly needs a way out, who needs something to do. Such people cannot remain inactive. The thirst for life, no matter what kind of life, as long as it comes now, as quickly as possible, leads them to absurdities, to the breaking of their souls and even to complete destruction."[19]

The thirst for life and for quick action are expressed in the idea which Raskolnikov seems to have developed. It appears, however, that instead of having mastered the idea, the idea has mastered our hero. He has become a blind tool of his own notion. His realization of failure and his first doubts about the correctness of his ideas are the initial signs of his return to life. Raskolnikov's human qualities, his compassion for the suffering and his concern for the well-being of man and society, are, according to Dostoevsky, the foundations on which Raskolnikov will build his new life. And even though, at that moment, he does "not believe in life hereafter,"[20] he is still redeemable; there is still hope for him.

It appears thus that the psychological make up of Raskolnikov's character facilitates, and the compositional plan for the novel requires, his survival. Had Raskolnikov committed suicide, the ideological message expressed in his regeneration would not have been possible; that is, the principle of atonement for one's sins through suffering could not have been illustrated. In addition, without Raskolnikov's expiation, the role of Sonia as a Christian martyr and saviour could not have been put into effect, and the contradictory duality of Raskolnikov's nature, his soul searching and quest for the truth, could not have been fully investigated and portrayed.

Svidrigailov

Raskolnikov's contemplated suicide alternates constantly with the idea of confession and surrender; it may also be viewed as a means of escaping just punishment which the defeated hero is reluctant to face. In the case of Svidrigailov suicide is seldom mentioned in the novel. Unlike Raskolnikov, Svidrigailov is not a criminal in the conventional sense. There is no need for him to hide from the pursuit of the law. And yet, the idea of escaping reality, which leads to his physical self-destruction, haunts him from the very first appearance on the pages of the novel. In fact, Svidrigailov's arrival in Petersburg is also, in a sense, an escape — he runs away from the countryside where he is haunted by the ghost of his dead wife. Svidrigailov's intended escape is identified in the beginning with a journey in an unspecified direction. Later it evolves into a projected journey to America, which becomes, in the final analysis, a metaphor for Svidrigailov's final escape from this world. At first Svidrigailov refers to America as the destination for his intended escape with Dunia. He also offers money to Raskolnikov so that he can run away to America in order to avoid persecution. In the end, when no one wants to join him on his journey, he shoots himself, thus embarking alone on his final trip to a so-called America from which there is no return. He tells a little Jewish-looking man in a soldier's greatcoat and an Achilles helmet, who is the only witness to his suicide, that he is "going to foreign parts ... to America."[21]

Svidrigailov enters the novel as a mysterious figure who is ready for final retribution. In one of the early drafts of *Crime and Punishment* Dostoevsky planned a conclusion to Svidrigailov's life which was vastly different from that described in the final version of the novel. Instead of having Svidrigailov deliberate, dream, and give away his money before his death, Dostoevsky has him spending his last night in debauchery after which he shoots himself. Such an ending would have placed Svidrigailov's past in a clearer perspective and it would have diminished the ambivalence and duality of his character. But Dostoevsky decided against such a conclusion and Svidrigailov's past and his depravity are mostly illustrated through the help of a number of literary devices such as flashbacks, dreams, insinuations and allusions, all of which help to shroud his personality in a cloak of mystery.

The idea of Raskolnikov's suicide recurs in the novel time and again, and yet few, including the reader, believe that Raskolnikov will actually kill himself. Porfiry Petrovich is positive that Raskolnikov is incapable of such an act. Svidrigailov thinks that Raskolnikov "may become a great rogue in time ... but now he want to live *too much!*"[22] The idea of Svidrigailov's suicide, on the other hand, develops slowly in the novel but it is structurally anticipated in the history of Svidrigailov's past and by the fate of those who surround this demonic mysterious figure. Svidrigailov's act of violent self-destruction is preceded by the suicides of his alleged victims. The story of the deaf-dumb girl of fourteen or fifteen, a distant relation of Mrs. Resslikh and the story of Philip the serf, are related by Luzhin, a man of questionable reputation. The truthfulness and reliability of these stories may be questioned; nevertheless they shed some light on the nature of Svidrigailov's personality, and they make his past seem even more enigmatic. We learn from Luzhin's stories that the girl had been brutally abused by Svidrigailov and driven to suicide.

Similarly, Philip had been driven to suicide by Svidrigailov's "ceaseless systematic persecution and punishment."[23] Both hung themselves. In his last dream Svidrigailov recognizes another of his possible victims. A girl of no more than fourteen, violated and savagely wounded, is driven to suicide by drowning. Dunia accuses Svidrigailov of another hideous crime. She tells him without hesitation: "You poisoned your wife ... you are a murderer."[24]

Thus Svidrigailov casts a grotesque and monstrous image of the oppressor surrounded by his victims, three of whom have been driven to suicide, two of these being adolescent girls. But Svidrigailov does not necessarily consider himself an oppressor. At the very first encounter with Raskolnikov, he asks: "Am I a monster or am I myself a victim?"[25] A victim of his own boredom and indifference, Svidrigailov is a man who has "no confidence in anything but anatomy."[26] He is a man who has lost his sense of moral values and for whom there is nothing beyond the immediate gratification of his perverted sensual passions and desires. Svidrigailov is aware of the fact that he is unable to control or satisfy the irrational cravings of his dissolute nature. He tells Raskolnikov that "reason, you know, is passion's slave; perhaps,after all, it was myself I did most harm!"[27] Indeed, a passion is seldom satisfied completely because as soon as it reaches the highest point of satisfaction it appears to stabilize, seeming to bring about the beginning of a decline in the intensity of fulfillment. This is perhaps why, at their last meeting, Svidrigailov does not abuse Dunia and sets her free. He realizes that she will satisfy his passion for a while only, and that he is doomed because his unquenchable thirst for sensual gratification is endless and irrational.

It is possible to suggest that the fateful encounter of Svidrigailov with Dunia, when he invites death by challenging her to shoot him, is a prelude to his final act of self-destruction. It appears that Dunia's refusal to accept Svidrigailov's declaration of love and his offer to save her brother, seal Svidrigailov's fate. Life becomes totally meaningless to him. He is even ready to accept death at the hands of his intended victim. V.Ia. Kirpotin suggests that Svidrigailov is not a profligate by nature, but that he turns to debauchery as to his last salvation from a life without meaning.[28] It appears thus that his sensual passion for Dunia is Svidrigailov's last escape from boredom, ennui and idleness. When Dunia rejects his advances, Svidrigailov, whose spirit has been dead long since, is prepared to face total physical annihilation.

The idea that Svidrigailov is not totally evil is also advanced by Iu.G. Kudriavtsev who asserts that "there is a ninety nine per cent of certainty that Svidrigailov is a criminal, yet one per cent of doubt remains. His unselfishness, his ability to help others, and the fact that he is not without honour confirm this one per cent of doubt."[29] Kudriavtsev goes even further by making the questionable assertion that Svidrigailov "is able to love deeply, and that life had meaning for him only as long as there was hope for reciprocal love."[30] Svidrigailov's suicide confirms, according to Kudriavtsev, his individuality, because only a real man can take his own life when it is threatened by nothing more than the meaninglessness of his existence.[31]

Vladimir Chizh, a professor of psychiatry, a researcher in experimental psychology and one of the early students of Dostoevsky's art, regards Svidrigailov as one of the best characters created by Dostoevsky. Chizh claims that Svidrigailov does not set Dunia free out of any sense of ethical or moral considerations, rather he argues that even a rake such as Svidrigailov requires and expects reciprocity in love and Svidrigailov realizes that all that Dunia feels for him is aversion and repugnance. Chizh suggests that "Svidrigailov's seeming large-heartedness is the result of his oversaturation */peresyshchen-nost'/*. A natural solution to such a life is suicide, because there is nothing to keep him attached to life. There are no desires, no interests, nothing in the future. Svidrigailov squanders his money and dies, giving no thought, in the last minutes, to his children."[32]

Svidrigailov has no friends to think of before his death. He has no one to bid farewell to. He dies totally indifferent to all, even to himself. Svidrigailov is not a stupid man. He is ready to admit to his failings but he realizes that he is helpless. As Richard Peace suggests, he "commits suicide because he realizes that the question he first put to Raskolnikov has been answered: he is *both* monster and victim, *both* oppressor and oppressed."[33] According to this explanation Svidrigailov is a tragic hero unable to come to terms with the internal duality of his own personality. He is a hero with positive impulses who is capable of good and selfless deeds which are, however, totally overshadowed by evil forces which guide and dominate his actions. He is a man who, when driven by his insatiable desires for sensual pleasures, does not have the ability to control himself or to make a rational distinction between good and evil.

Philip Rahv suggests that "Svidrigailov exemplifies a distinct character-type in Dostoevsky, the type of the nihilist in the realm of sensuality.... In this character-type, sensuality becomes a flight from the vertiginous consciousness of freedom and from a kind of ennui which has gone beyond the psychological and has acquired a metaphysical status."[34] Thus, Svidrigailov rejects all dogma, but he believes in ghosts. He tells Raskolnikov that as soon as man "falls ill ... the possibility of another world begins to appear, and as the illness increases, so do the contacts with the other world."[35] Svidrigailov speculates about the possibility of a future life, an eternity which he conceives of as "one little room, something like a bath-house in the country, black with soot, with spiders in every corner."[36] In admitting to his illness Svidrigailov, by his own definition, closes in on this uninviting eternity. His disease is his debauchery, "like everything else that goes to extremes." Svidrigailov refuses to give it up, because according to him, it is "based on nature, indeed, and not subject to fantasy, something that exists in the blood as an eternal flame."

Svidrigailov agrees "that a respectable man is morally obliged to put up with boredom,"[37] and although he does not consider himself moral, he clings to life. When asked by Raskolnikov whether he could shoot himself, Svidrigailov turns away with an expression of aversion and he says: "Do me a favour, and don't speak of that ... I confess to an unpardonable weakness, but I can't help it: I am afraid of death and don't like to hear it spoken of."[38] Svidrigailov's conversations with Raskolnikov uncover the extreme dichotomy of the former's nature. "He has an absolute lust for life and is afraid of death, yet he demands death as the ultimate sign of the self's free mastery, the conquest of his last fear, and the vindication of his freedom."[39]

Svidrigailov is often described as a strong man who can find no positive outlet for his strength, which therefore becomes self-destructive. It is often said that "his evil lies precisely in his denial of his generous impulses and in his cynical refusal to follow the inclinations of his conscience."[40] Indeed Svidrigailov is strong when it is necessary to act, but he is utterly weak in restraint. The only time that he does not manage to restrain himself and act in a manner contrary to his irrational impulses, is in his last encounter with Dunia. Restraint and self-control do not come easily to him. Dostoevsky writes that "there was in Svidrigailov's soul an instant of terrible, silent struggle."[41] He gives Dunia the key without looking at her and asks here to leave immediately. He knows that when he is in a fit of sensual passion he cannot control himself, he is not responsible for his actions. But Dostoevsky does not justify totally restrained self-will or totally unrestrained passion. In neither instance does Dostoevsky absolve man of responsibility for his actions. Man is to go on living, bearing simultaneously the terrible burden of his nature and of his personal freedom.

Thus Svidrigailov the oppressor is turned into a victim of his own nature and destiny: he is haunted by the ghosts of his dead victims and he is hated even by those whom he professes to love and to want to help in good faith. The world seems to be full of people but Svidrigailov faces death in total loneliness, alienated from, and rejected by, all. There is no room in this world for a superman who does not put his strength to good use.

Symbolically even nature rises against Svidrigailov. He is accompanied on his last journey by a blustering and whistling wind and a stormy river. According to George Gibian, "water is to Dostoevsky a symbol of rebirth and regeneration.... By the same token the significance of water may be the opposite to negative characters. Water holds the terror of death for the corrupt Svidrigailov."[42] He selects a day of cold and rain to put an end to himself. He walks by little houses which look dirty and dejected. He meets the little Jewish soldier who tries to drive Svidrigailov away by saying "but you can't do that here! This is not the proper place!"[43] — as if there were a proper place to kill oneself.

Svidrigailov's suicide is the final act of individual self-will by a man who refuses, and is unable, to accept suffering on his path to spiritual salvation. It is a symbolic condemnation of a way of life which ignores moral human values and advocates ethical corruption. It is a warning to those who seek a meaning in life outside the Christian principles of the Russian Church, and, in particular, to Raskolnikov who has yet to choose between suicide and surrender, between continuous rebellion and humility. Raskolnikov survives because he has his roots in the Russian soil. He refuses to go to "America." Svidrigailov is rootless and, therefore, according to Dostoevsky, he is doomed. Without relations or friends, withouts roots in his native land which could support him in case of need, life becomes meaningless and tiresome. Man cannot exist in a physical and spiritual vacuum without a clear objective in life. Svidrigailov has no ties with his land or with its people and, therefore, there is no room for him in this Russian world.

Dostoevsky painstakingly prepares Svidrigailov's path to self-destruction. From the moment of his first appearance on the pages of the novel he is constantly moving closer to his final destination. And yet, a number of notable scholars are critical of Dostoevsky's treatment of this character and are sceptical about his suicide. E.H. Carr, for example, suggests that

"Svidrigailov is evidently an afterthought," who "makes his first appearance exactly half-way through the novel.... He remains to the last a mysterious figure, a symbol rather than a man."[44] Carr asserts further that Dunia's release is "incompatible with the principle of unrestrained self-indulgence,"[45] and that Svidrigailov's "suicide remains obscure and ineffective. We are doubtless intended to infer the moral bankruptcy of hedonism; but the point is not well made. The truth is that it was necessary to remove Svidrigailov rather hurriedly from the stage in order to leave it free for the closing scene of Raskolnikov's tragedy."[46] Similarly, Victor Shklovsky propounds a view that Dostoevsky complicates and almost poeticizes the image of Svidrigailov in the end of the novel. He claims that "Svidrigailov the card-sharper, profligate, and oppressor, saves all before his death. Otherwise ends do not meet."[47] Yet Shklovsky asserts also that the image of Svidrigailov symbolizes "the total freedom from ethical prohibitions, given to the villain, who does not recognize anything beyond his personal desires,"[48] alluding thus to the fact that Svidrigailov's physical death is the result of his moral transgressions.

Not all scholars agree with the views of Carr and Shklovsky. V.Ia. Kirpotin makes an attempt to refute the idea that Svidrigailov's character is introduced into the novel for the sole purpose of moving the plot. Kirpotin suggests that such a view is "incorrect in regard to the novel and to Dostoevsky himself. Dostoevsky, the great master of plot construction, could certainly have found another solution to the plot, without a card-sharper or a poisoner-benefactor."[49] Of course, Dostoevsky could have created another hero, with other personal traits, instead of Svidrigailov. Judging by the early drafts of the novel, there are indications that he wanted to do so; however there is no definite proof that those who were to replace the Svidrigailov who appears in the novel would be artistically more viable than the Svidrigailov we know.

In conclusion it is possible to suggest that structurally and symbolically Svidrigailov's suicide is well-prepared. It is also metaphysically substantiated. Svidrigailov's death is perhaps psychologically not quite convincing, giving rise to the critique that Dostoevsky had to remove him from the scene in order to be able to lead the novel to its logical conclusion. After all, Svidrigailov is not a "logical" suicide who is out to prove something by destroying himself. He readily admits that he loves life and its pleasures not less than any other human being. Even to a strong and self-willed man such as Svidrigailov, death should certainly not be a laughing matter, and one may continue to wonder about Svidrigailov's state of mind when he jokingly pulls the trigger of his gun. One may joke about someone else's death, but very seldom about one's own.

It is apparent that with certain reservations the suicide of Svidrigailov is well integrated with the structural development of his character and not merely a device applied in the novel with the sole purpose of removing the hero from the scene. But most importantly the suicide of Svidrigailov illustrates Dostoevsky's ethical conception of life. It is a symbolic example that man cannot escape punishment for the violation of the accepted but unwritten moral laws which govern the interaction of man in a social environment. It is an indication that unlimited freedom and self-will lead to corruption and the disintegration of the personality and that spiritual stagnation is self-destructive and can lead to total physical annihilation.

Dostoevsky's approach to his subject matter is selective. He chooses, in each instance, the material which he considers most appropriate for a given situation. In his notebooks Dostoevsky even considers Marmeladov committing suicide by drowning himself, but decides against such a solution because the weak-willed civil servant allegedly has "no guts"[50] for such a decisive step. Indeed, the character of Marmeladov is not given the necessary determination to end his life by a willful and violent act; he destroys himself slowly and recklessly by succumbing to the temptation of alcohol and meets his death, crushed by horses, under the wheels of a carriage.

The evolution of Dostoevsky's conception of the character of Marmeladov makes it unnecessary, if not impossible, for him to commit suicide. Despite the fact that his addiction to drink leads to the destruction and misery of his family and drives Sonia into the street by forcing her to turn to prostitution in order to be able to support his wife's children, Marmeladov is perceived as a positive character from a Christian point of view. He is selfless and compassionate; he is overwhelmed by a sense of guilt; and, he repents for his sins. He asks forgiveness from those whom he offends and is ready to suffer for his transgressions. Indeed, the weak Marmeladov has no "guts." In the final version of the novel he needs the strength to fight his addiction rather than to kill himself. As it is, life for him is hell, and, therefore, as a believing Christian, he can be saved from suffering by death. Suicide, for Dostoevsky, is the prerogative of nihilists and unbelievers, and Marmeladov is not one of them.

There is another incident of attempted suicide in *Crime and Punishment* which is connected with one of its numerous subplots. The painter Nikolai Dement'ev (Mikolka), who at the time of the murder works in one of the flats below the apartment of Alena Ianovna, finds a jeweller's case with gold earrings in it, apparently lost by Raskolnikov, and he pawns it for a drink. When he is suspected in the murder and pursued, he runs away and attempts to hang himself because he is very much afraid that he will be condemned for the crime.[51] During the interrogation Mikolka, who is a schismatic and who has spent some time under the direct guidance of an elder, takes upon himself the crime and admits to the murder of the two women.

At first sight it might appear that the incident with Mikolka, the painter, is only a melodramatic device introduced by the author in order to complicate the plot and heighten the element of suspense in the novel. Upon closer scrutiny, however, it becomes possible to accept L. Grossman's suggestion that the subconscious moral power of Nikolai Dement'ev opposes and counteracts the "theoretical" notions of Raskolnikov, a man who is alienated from the soil and who commits a crime in order to prove a point.[52]

The character of Mikolka is modelled after one of the schismatic convicts depicted in the *House of the Dead.*[53] In a way it foreshadows the predicament of Dmitrii Karamazov. Mikolka is not guilty of any crime, yet he is ready to accept suffering, not suffering for somebody's sake, but suffering as a necessity.[54] A.L. Bem asserts that the episode with Mikolka is "closely connected with the problem of guilt which is the main idea of the novel," because the desire to suffer "cannot be explained without the assumption that the feeling of original guilt has been planted in man's soul."[55] It appears thus that Dostoevsky places the simple peasant Mikolka on an ethical level above that of the educated Raskolnikov: the former is able to share the guilt of his fellow man and is ready to suffer for him, while the latter rejects his guilt and attempts to justify his crime.

According to the above critical opinions, Dostoevsky introduces the character of Nikolai Dement'ev with the primary purpose of contrasting his personality and predicament with the fate of Raskolnikov. The comparison of the two heroes also brings to the reader's attention a number of problems which the writer develops further in his later novels. Dostoevsky alludes here, for example, to the notion that man is both good and evil, that the source of goodness in man is in his irrational heart rather than in his rational mind, that those who have lost their roots are doomed to spiritual stagnation, and that the readiness to accept guilt and suffer for the sake of others is the highest expression of man's affinity and identification with his fellow man.

2. THE IDIOT (IDIOT, 1868)

There are no less than eight different versions of the first draft of *The Idiot*, but from its very early drafts, motives of murder and suicide are often intertwined, and irrational self-destructive instincts determine the destinies of almost all important protagonists.[1]

Most important for the philosophical conception of the novel is the character of Ippolit Terent'ev and his attempted suicide. Ippolit's story dominates the middle part of the novel and his rebellion against the dark forces of nature unites the revolt of the underground man with the rebellion of Ivan Karamazov. In his *Notebooks for "The Idiot"* Dostoevsky envisages Ippolit as the "main axis of the whole novel";[2] a man who has hold over most other protagonists. According to N.N. Chirkov, Ippolit's confession is "the most important place in the novel, the focus, where all its basic motives meet."[3] In his confession Ippolit attempts to give a rational explanation to his worldview and to justify his intended suicide.

The first thought of suicide comes to Ippolit when he stands with his school friend Bakhmutov on the Neva bridge, leaning with his elbows on the balustrade and looking into the river. At that time he lacks the necessary resolve for such a decisive step.[4] His final decision to kill himself is influenced by several incidents which place his position and his perception of life in a new perspective. On one occasion Ippolit sees a strange dream in which a poisonous, dreadful-looking creature, resembling a scorpion, enters his room. A battle between his dog Norma and the scorpion ensues. Just as the dog is cracking the scorpion's shell between her teeth, the horrible creature succeeds in stinging her tongue. This dream symbolizes man's struggle with the dark forces of evil which are inherenet in the natural world.

On another occasion Ippolit is profoundly affected by the sight of Holbein's picture of Christ's deposition from the cross which he observes in Rogozhin's apartment. The picture shocks him. The dead body of Christ looks the same as the corpse of any man after such suffering. Gazing at the picture Ippolit says, "you get the impression of nature as some enormous, implacable, and dumb beast, or, to put it more correctly ... as some huge engine of the latest design, which has senselessly seized, cut to pieces, and swallowed up — impassively and unfeelingly — a great and priceless Being, a Being worth the whole of nature and all its laws."[5] The picture kills whatever faith Ippolit has by making him aware of his insignificance. It also gives a symbolic explanation of the power of nature which trapped him. He questions: "if death is so horrible and if the laws of nature are so powerful, then how can they be overcome?"[6] The picture suggests to Ippolit the idea of a dark, insolent, senseless and omnipotent eternal power which controls all; it is an idea which overwhelms his being and makes him unconsciously aware of his own weakness and inferiority; it is a notion which makes him realize his limitations and insignificance in relation to the dark forces of nature. Ippolit's final decision to commit suicide is also influenced by another dream. He remembers that in the dream someone with a lighted candle seemed to lead him by the hand, showing him some huge and horrible tarantula and assuring him that it was the dark, deaf-and-dumb and all powerful creature.

Thus the picture of Christ at Rogozhin's and the symbolic dreams of the scorpion and the tarantula merge into one, and cause Ippolit to finally make up his mind. As he admits, it is "not logic, not a logical conviction, but disgust that helped me to arrive at my final decision. It is impossible to go on living when life assumes such grotesque and humiliating forms ... I cannot submit to a dark power which assumes the form of a tarantula."[7]

Ippolit is not an atheist. He admits to the existence of eternal life, but his faith, as K. Mochulsky suggests, "is not Christian, but *philosophical*."[8] Ippolit claims total ignorance in the ways of Providence. He says that he cannot be blamed for failing to understand the incomprehensible. He cannot accept true Christian obedience, as it is exemplified in the image of Prince Myshkin. He refuses to accept a world order which he does not understand and cannot change. In this sense Ippolit anticipates Ivan Karamazov who does not reject God but refuses to accept God's world.

Suicide is the only act that Ippolit claims to be able to begin and to end of his own free will. The intended suicide is an act of despair and of defiance against the laws of nature which are totally indifferent to his desires and wishes. It is an expression of his self-assertion and self-will as opposed to the Christian submission advocated by the prince. Ippolit's situation is hopeless because he is soon doomed to die of consumption anyway. He refuses to be a "piano key," that is, he wants to die with dignity and he challenges nature by trying to disrupt the normal course of his natural life in willfully putting and end to himself.

Ippolit is a tragic figure. He seeks martyrdom, yet, as E.H. Carr suggests, he actually "never quite grips us,"[9] because his thinking is sometimes confused and contradictory. Like most of Dostoevsky's rational intellectuals, Ippolit is torn apart by inner doubts and contrariety. He is spiteful, bitter and self-centred. He helps others, not from altrusitic inclinations but in order to gain the respect and admiration of those he comes in touch with. E. Wasiolek suggests that Ippolit's "confession is rife with self-glorification: ... he compares himself to Christ in his frustrating impotence before nature. His image of frustrated heroism is naive and taken from sentimental novels."[10] Wasiolek asserts further that there is no reason to doubt Ippolit's sincerity in his confession. It is a fact, however, that according to Dostoevsky, no matter how sincere Ippolit's intentions are, he cannot do anything good for humanity because as an intellectual humanist he can only assume the gesture of heroism rather than being a real hero. Wasiolek claims that

> *"Ippolit embodies one of Dostoevsky's most important ideas: a corrupted nature (and a corrupted nature is one that believes in itself, and not in God) corrupts everything it touches, no matter how noble, good, sympathetic, and grand it may appear."*[11]

On the metaphysical plane Ippolit is a rebel who refuses to accept the established order of things. In ordinary daily life, however, Ippolit is a sick man who refuses to accept the unavoidable and who questions the justice of his impending death. Ippolit wants very much to live and his revolt is, in a sense, a rebellion against the destructive potentialities of nature which chooses at random whom and when to strike. In fact, Ippolit's rebellion is against the inevitability of death, more precisely against his own death. It is paradoxical that the tool of rebellion, the instrument which is to counteract and defy the verdict of nature and its death sentence, is suicide, that is, the same death. Ippolit wants to overcome the forces of death with death, while Dostoevsky suggests that only the forces of real life can overcome death. According to Dostoevsky, faith in eternal life and in the immortality of the soul are the tools which one is to seek on one's way to the conquest of physical death and to spiritual salvation.

There are indications in the notebooks for the novel that Dostoevsky was himself not sure whether to keep Ippolit alive or to have him killed.[12] In the final version of the novel Ippolit's attempted suicide fails. The gun does not misfire, but Ippolit has apparently forgotten to place a firing cap in his pistol, turning his attempted self-destruction into a painful farce. On the psychological plane the attempted suicide fails because Ippolit's desire to live is very strong. Ippolit says that the idea "that it is not worth while living for a few weeks began, I think, to take hold of me in good earnest a month ago, when I had only four weeks to live."[13] Until then, in spite of being aware of his incurable illness, he still clings to life. Ippolit admits that the more clearly he understands his hopeless position, the more desperately he wants to live. On the philosophical plane it is possible to suggest that Dostoevsky saves Ippolit because his death would prove nothing. Ippolit defies death, just as Kirillov does, but he is not out to prove anything, as Kirillov is. The notebooks for *The Idiot* make it clear that Dostoevsky sees Ippolit's suicide as an act of vanity, the "vanity of a weak character."[14]

It seems quite plausible that Ippolit attempts suicide because he wants to impress those who are listening to his confession. As a matter of fact, Radomsky suggests that "I've never seen it actually happen that a man should deliberately shoot himself to gain admiration or out of spite because he was not admired."[15] It is estimated "that seventy-five per cent of successful and would-be suicides give clear warning of their intentions beforehand, and are often driven to act because their warnings are ignored and brushed aside or, like Mayakovsky's, treated as mere bravado. At a certain point of despair a man will kill himself in order to show he is serious. It is also estimated that a person who has once been to the brink is perhaps three times more likely to go there again than someone who has not. Suicide is like diving off a high board: the first time is the worst."[16] Ippolit has been to the brink. He tries to dive off the high board. He does not succeed, and although he could try to kill himself again, he never does.

Erwin Stengel, the noted neuropsychiatrist and psychoanalyst, suggests that "most people who commit suicidal acts want either to die or to live; they want to do both at the same time, usually the one more or much more, than the other."[17] Ippolit wants to live much more than he wants to die, and, therefore, he fails in his suicide attempt. He submits to fate and later dies a natural death. It is possible only to surmise that Ippolit's attempted suicide is a philosophical decision rather than a psychological necessity. In the notebooks to the novel Prince Myshkin suggests that Ippolit "won't kill himself now, having missed out on it, for it would make no impression on those people, so now he won't kill himself."[18] Ippolit's act could be viewed as a social communication, an attention-getter, a desperate cry for help. But the whole situation may also seem ironic, because had Ippolit's attempted suicide been successful, how could he witness and benefit from the admiration and attention of those who remained alive and well.

Ippolit, one of the major characters in the novel, is important for the understanding of the ideational essence of the narrative, but his image could be regarded as secondary to the development of the main plot. Ippolit makes his first appearance only in the author's late plans for the novel. In fact, "in the most serious and sophisticated sense, Ippolit is an afterthought, an elaboration or refinement of the core situation."[19] It appears that the emergence of Ippolit is prompted by the development of the central drama in the novel which evolves around the fates of its main protagonists, whose destinies are intertwined in two love triangles which form the structural and thematic foundation of *The Idiot.*

Four people are involved in the two love triangles: Prince Myshkin, Rogozhin, Nastasiia Filippovna, and Aglaia. All of them meet a disastrous end. In the beginning of the novel, Myshkin and Parfion Rogozhin travel in the same train compartment on their way to Petersburg. They discuss Rogozhin's infatuation with the notorious Nastasiia Filippovna Barashkov, foreshadowing the formation of the first triangle. The other triangle, composed of Myshkin, Aglaia and Nastasiia Filippovna is formed somewhat later, but it is closely linked to, and influenced by, the development of the first one.

The love triangle is a device which allows the author to probe and uncover the essential traits of character of his heroes. But as the fates of many protagonists in the novel illustrate, a love triangle is a state of human relationships in which self-destructive elements are prevalent. No satisfactory solution is possible to a conflict in a love triangle because self-serving, irrational impulses, generated by passionate emotions of love and hate, dominate reason and common sense.

Thus, Nastasiia Filippovna is murdered by Rogozhin. All the way through the novel she is pursued by a presentiment of inevitable death. Her final escape with Rogozhin is essentially a suicidal act. Intuition tells her that Rogozhin's passion is murderous, yet she follows him blindly after her escape from Myshkin. Nastasiia Filippovna is attracted by the spiritual purity of the Prince, but she cannot accept his forgiveness and feels unworthy of him. E. Wasiolek asks a pointed question: "What does Nastasya Fillipovna want?" and he answers that "*As payment for her hurt, she wants to be hurt again.*" "Nastasya loves her disgrace (*pozor*) more than she loves the innocence that the Prince embodies and offers her. Her living hurt is the flame in which her self burns and glows."[20] Nastasiia Filippovna is a proud humiliated woman who is forced to play a role she is not suited for. She turns away all suitors and rejects all logical solutions for a secure future. She is hurt but unable to forgive those who abused her. She is ready to suffer rather than to compromise.

Symbolically, before her death Nastasiia Filippovna reads the French novel *Madame Bovary*, and perhaps compares her own fate with the fate of Flaubert's Emma, who poisons herself. Nastasiia Filippovna could never become an adultress like Madame Bovary because at heart she is pure.[21] In the early drafts of the novel, plans for Nastasiia's death alternate with plans for her suicide. At one point we are told that "she dies or kills herself."[22] In another place we read that "she wants to throw herself into the water."[23] It is apparent that the "fallen woman" who has been disgraced in her youth through no fault of her own, is doomed from the very beginning. She cannot become a new Nastasiia Filippovna because she cannot forget the old one. She loves, as Wasiolek suggests, her disgrace, yet she destroys herself because she cannot live in a state of constant degradation. She is torn apart by internal contradictions. This inner dichotomy prevents her from adapting to changing life conditions and obscures her vision in a world full of evil and corruption, leading to her downfall and ultimate destruction.

The other members of the two love triangles are also destroyed. The Prince's delicate nature and weak health cannot withstand the clash between his ideal world and the terrible world of reality. His selfless and compassionate character cannot contend with the tragic intensity of events in which he becomes unexpectedly enveloped. The novel ends with Myshkin and Rogozhin keeping vigil over the dead corpse of Nastasiia Filippovna, Myshkin having reverted to a mental state which many years before resulted in his admission to Schneider's mental clinic in Switzerland. Thus the circle closes. At first, having at least partially recuperated from his illness, Myshkin returns to Russia with high hopes for a bright future. In the end he is taken back to Switzerland in a state of total mental disintegration.

The third member of the first triangle, Rogozhin, is also ruined. He is found at the dead body of Nastasiia Filippovna in a raging fever and completely unconscious. He survives two months of inflammation of the brain and, when he recovers, he is sentenced to fifteen years hard labour in Siberia. Rogozhin is driven to murder by self-destructive jealousy. His love is an irrational desire, but he is not a simple pleasure seeker. His passion is a power which he cannot control and therefore, it is destructive.

The third member of the second triangle, Aglaia Epanchin, is a young innocent girl, but she is also capricious, sarcastic, and sometimes malicious. In the beginning though she makes fun of Myshkin, she is irritated that he does not treat her as all other men do. She is attracted by his spiritual qualities and puzzled by an inner feeling which irresistibly draws her towards him. Aglaia's fateful encounter with Nastasiia Filippovna affords a terrible blow to her aspirations and vanity. It also dispels her illusions about her love for Myshkin, because, as Radomsky says, "Aglaya loved like a woman, like a human being, and not like — a disembodied spirit."[24] Aglaia's predicament and the tragic conclusion to Myshkin's brief appearance in Russia have a devastating effect on her fate. She tries to escape from her problems by seeking fulfilment in other quarters. She marries a Polish émigré who pretends to be a rich count but who turns out to be a poor individual of dubious reputation. Aglaia is a young woman capable of strong emotions. When she realizes that Myshkin is in no position to satisfy her yearnings, she throws herself on the mercy of those who can, at least temporarily, quench her thirst for emotional and spiritual fulfilment, apparently mistaking the probable for the real.

In the end, all four protagonists are destroyed: Nastasiia Filippovna is dead, Rogozhin is imprisoned, Myshkin reverts to a state of total mental collapse, and Aglaia, whose emotional stability is shattered, faces an uncertain future. The conclusion of the novel is not a happy one. So much human potential is wasted, so much energy is expended to no use. All this destruction is self-inflicted because the protagonists fail to master their passions and control their desires. They are unable to adapt to a reality which is alien to their natures, setting goals for themselves which are doomed to failure.

The only actual suicide mentioned in *The Idiot* is of little significance to the general composition of the novel. It is reported first by Nastasiia Filippovna and later by General Epanchin that Kapiton Alekseevich, the uncle of Evgenii Pavlovich Radomsky, has squandered a large amount of public money and shot himself.[25] We know little about the background of Kapiton Alekseevich; he does not appear in person on the pages of the novel. It seems that Nastasiia Filippovna uses the incident of Kapiton Alekseevich's suicide to embarass Radomsky in the eyes of the Epanchin girls, a step obviously connected with her designs on the fates of Aglaia and Myshkin. In the early drafts and notes to the novel Radomsky and his uncle appear under the names of Vel'monchek and Politkovsky accordingly.[26] The prototype for Radomsky's uncle is the high government official Aleksandr Gavrilovich Politkovsky who served the tsar Nicholas I, embezzled over a million rubles and poisoned himself.[27] In the early drafts of *The Idiot* the uncle's means of suicide alternate between poisoning, as Politkovsky does in real life, and shooting himself, as is the fate of Radomsky's uncle in the final version of the novel.[28]

Radomsky's (Vel'monchek's) uncle is not the only character to commit suicide in Dostoevsky's early plans for the novel. Vel'monchek himself, who at one stage in the development of the novel is to marry Lebedev's daughter, shoots himself "out of vanity"[29] and because of his debts. In another version he shoots himself after having taken upon himself the guilt for stealing 1700 rubles from Lebedev, money which has been actually stolen by the General (Ivolgin). In the final version of the narrative, with the exception of the reported case of Kapiton Alekseevich, no actual suicides are described. Thus *The Idiot* is the only major novel by Dostoevsky in which not s single important character is successful in taking his own life.

3. "THE ETERNAL HUSBAND (VECHNYI MUZH, 1870)

The theme of "The Eternal Husband," one of Dostoevsky's great minor works, is connected in spirit with the major novels which precede and follow it. Love triangles are at the compositional centre of *The Insulted and Injured*, of *The Idiot* and of *The Brothers Karamazov*. A variation of the same theme is presented in "The Eternal Husband." Nine years have passed since the love affair between Aleksei Ivanovich Vel'chaninov and Natal'ia Vasil'evna Trusotsky has been terminated. It is only after the death of Natal'ia Vasil'evna that her deceived husband, Pavel Pavlovich, finds out that his wife has been unfaithful to him. He also discovers that after Vel'chaninov she had another lover, Bagautov and that his child, the girl Liza, is not his child after all, but rather that of Vel'chaninov. After his wife's death, Trusotsky comes with Liza to Petersburg with the alleged purpose of taking revenge on his wife's lovers. There he learns that Bagautov is dead, but he finds Vel'chaninov and attempts to slash his throat with a razor.

One of the main themes of "The Eternal Husband" is the investigation of the spiritual link between two men who love the same woman. The dominant idea of mutual repulsion is paralleled in the story with the motif of mutual attraction. Dostoevsky examines the complex love-hate relationship between the "eternal husband," Trusotsky and the "eternal lover," Vel'chaninov.

There is only one actual suicide in "The Eternal Husband" which outwardly does not appear to be connected with the main plot of the story. Upon closer scrutiny, however, it becomes evident that murder-suicide motif is the underlying mainspring propelling the development of the plot. The suicide of a certain nameless clerk is reported to Vel'chaninov by Mar'ia Sysoevna, the landlady of Trusotsky's lodging. The clerk squanders all his money and hangs himself. When Pavel Pavlovich returns home, apparently a little drunk, he finds a frightened Liza and learns that she witnessed the suicide, which has thrown her into a terrible shock. Liza is now a perfect object upon whom Pavel Pavlovich can vent his own frustrations. He terrorizes the girl by threatening to hang himself, and produces a cord with which he would make a noose before her eyes. The threats of her father drive Liza to madness. Thinking that she must be guilty of something she begs his forgiveness. These threats are frequent and on one occasion, had it not been for Mar'ia Sysoevna, Liza might have thrown herself out of the window.[1]

Liza is attached to and loves Trusotsky dearly; she presumes that he is her real father. But Pavel Pavlovich, the cheated husband, who does not know until his wife's very death that he loves the child of a stranger, avenges himself on Vel'chaninov by tormenting and abusing Liza, and ultimately driving her to death. These threats instill such fear in Liza that when she is placed by Vel'chaninov with his friends, the Pogorel'tsevs, she remains convinced that in her absence her father might hang himself. Demanding to see her father, she relates to Vel'chaninov the scene with the cord. Liza believes that Pavel Pavlovich may indeed hang himself and that he always wanted to hang himself.[2]

Vel'chaninov is puzzled by Liza's words, yet the idea that Trusotsky might kill himself like the clerk in Mar'ia Sysoevna's story haunts him continuously. He realizes that had he been in Trusotsky's place he would perhaps have considered a similar act.[3] The notion of Pavel Pavlovich's possible suicide obsesses Val'chaninov to an extreme degree. When the young man, Lobov, comes with a message from Trusotsky (who is leaving town) and brings the fateful letter to Natal'ia Vasil'evna in which her relationship with Vel'chaninov is clarified, Vel'chaninov mutters mechanically to the amazed boy that Pavel Pavlovich must have hanged himself before actually realizing what he says.

In the early drafts of "The Eternal Husband" Trusotsky's suicidal intentions are less enigmatic than those expressed in its final version. The idea of Trusotsky's suicide appears in different combinations, but primarily in connection with his intent to avenge himself on his wife's lovers. At one point Trusotsky tells Vel'chaninov: "I have come here in order to hang myself — or to avenge myself; or, perhaps, to avenge myself and later hang myself; or, perhaps, just to hang myself, without taking revenge."[4] On another occasion Trusotsky tells Vel'chaninov that his urge to avenge himself on the high official (Bagautov) prevents him from destroying himself. He says that he "wanted to hang himself, but only *he* kept him from taking this step."[5]

Vel'chaninov is always sceptical of Trusotsky's intentions. In the early drafts for the story he suspects that Trusotsky may indeed avenge himself on his adversaries, but that he will fail later to carry out his intentions of hanging himself.[6] In a final note to the early drafts Dostoevsky alternates the notion of Trusotsky's suicide with the idea of his second marriage.[7] In the conclusion of the story we encounter Trustosky, in the company of his young wife, the provincial lady Olimpiada Semenovna (Lipochka) and the young lancer Miten'ka, whose presence points to a situation reminiscent of Trusotsky's previous position. His role as a cuckold and "eternal husband" is perpetuated.

I.Z. Serman suggests that Dostoevsky possibly turned to the subject of cuckoldry under the influence of Flaubert's novel *Madame Bovary* which he read upon the advice of Turgenev in 1867.[8] Emma Bovary, the unfaithful wife of Charles, poisons herself. Charles is driven to distraction by his terrible loss. When he finds the love letters of his wife's paramours, his life becomes totally shattered and fate deals him its final blow. His agony becomes unbearable and he dies from, what appears to be, excruciating grief.

From the early drafts of the story, the similarities between the fate of the Bovary family and the predicament of the Trusotskys are evident. In both cases the husbands trust and dearly love their wives. Both husbands learn about the deceit of their wives from love letters discovered after each death. In *Madame Bovary* Emma's suicide drives Charles to death. In the initial plans for "The Eternal Husband" Natal'ia Vasil'evna's death leads to Trusotsky's suicide. In the final version of "The Eternal Husband" Trustosky is spared in body, but he is destroyed in spirit. He is too indecisive and weak to be able to take his own life. He is a dreamer rather than a man of action and his physical annihilation is replaced by complete moral disintegration. Trusotsky again becomes a passive and credulous member of a new love triangle. He finds himself in a situation in which ethical corruption and the dissolution of his personality are inevitable. It is suggested that Trusotsky is one of Dostoevsky's most sophisticated and delicate masochists. He is a psychological cripple who courts cuckoldry which has become for him an emotional necessity.[9]

Initially the idea of Trusotsky's suicide is connected with the idea of murder. It reflects the classical murder-suicide scenario of a love triangle in which all members of the fateful trio perish. In "The Eternal Husband" the female partner is dead from the outset, and the deceived husband intends first to murder his male adversary and later kill himself. In fact, however,

Bagautov has died a natural death, and Vel'chaninov is spared from Trusotsky's evil intentions by fate. Thus, it might appear that since there is no murder, the suicide of Trusotsky which is to follow is also unnecessary. Although Dostoevsky abandons his early murder-suicide plans in which Trusotsky is the main active force, he does not dispense completely with his murder-suicide designs for the story. Trusotsky's intended suicide is replaced by the suicide of an insignificant secondary character which sets in motion the process leading to the destruction and death of Liza. The intended murder of Vel'chaninov is replaced by the death of Liza. Instead of killing Vel'chaninov Trusotsky avenges himself on his alleged enemy by destroying Liza, the symbol of Vel'chaninov's future. The suffering and death of an innocent child concurs with the motif of the wronged girl which is prevalent in many of Dostoevsky's other works.

Trusotsky, the perpetual cuckold, submits to the self-destructive forces of his nature. In fact, he may not even be aware of his downfall and the disintegration of his own personality. Vel'chaninov, on the other hand, may appear initially to be a strong hero. Yet the very beginning of "The Eternal Husband" which starts with an introduction and outline of his character, points to the contrary. In the past a libertine, Vel'chaninov is found in a state of mental anguish. He is subject to nervous depression. He reminisces and dreams about his past, in which he abused and offended many innocent people. Among others, he wronged a young girl of the working class and abandoned her with child without even saying good-bye. Many years later Vel'chaninov tries to find that girl but with no success. It appears that Vel'chaninov is haunted by his past. He is tormented by an inner sense of guilt which could turn into a devastating self-destructive force unless his guilty conscience is relieved.

According to A.L. Bem, the introduction to the story and Dostoevsky's method of narration in which reality, dream, and hallucination are closely intertwined make it difficult to distinguish between what is real and what is fantasy, between what actually happens in the story and what is the fiction of Vel'chaninov's morbid imagination. Bem suggests that "The Eternal Husband" is narrated on two different levels: "On the external level, the level of real-psychological narration, and on a deeper internal level which relates to the world of fantasy. Dostoevsky is not aware of the fact that both levels are parallel, creating thus a situation which makes possible to accept either on equal terms. *But the real understanding of his (Dostoevsky's) work is impossible without taking into consideration the main and deeper level of his creative work.*"[10] The whole story is, in Bem's view, an expression of Vel'chaninov's "tragedy of conscience"[11] where his present state of mind is induced by the awakening of his inner conscience, and by the sudden realization of his guilt.[12]

Bem believes that Vel'chaninov's guilty conscience craves punishment. It creates, therefore, the image of the eternal husband who is supposed to avenge himself on his wrong-doers. It is suggested that it is quite possible that the encounter betwen Vel'chaninov and Trusotsky, when the latter tries unsuccessfully to murder the former, never takes place at all and is rather the fiction of Vel'chaninov's imagination whose guilt-ridden conscience demands retribution. Notwithstanding Bem's hypothesis, Vel'chaninov does give reign to his self-destructive impulses by challenging fate and inviting disaster. He pursues a close relationship with Trusotsky who has come to Petersburg to avenge himself on his foes. Vel'chaninov is tempted to establish contact with Trusotsky because he senses correctly that Liza is his daughter. But it is not his fate to be father to a child he once abandoned. He fails in his attempt to trace his child by the young working girl and his contact with Liza is short-lived because of Trusotsky's vengeful nature.

Dostoevsky provides the protagonists of "The Eternal Husband" with the self-destructive traits characteristic of the heroes of his early fiction and combines them with the application of suicide and violent death as an artistic device intended to move the plot. Vel'chaninov, the libertine, who is allegedly obsessed with a guilt complex and Trusotsky, the passive dreamer and cuckold, have much in common with Dostoevsky's pre- and post-Siberian heroes. Although the suicide of the nameless clerk may appear to have little significance to the main plot, it triggers the actions of other important protagonists setting in motion the development of the narrative along the lines envisaged by the author.

4. THE POSSESSED (BESY, 1871-72)

More evil is unleashed, more destructive and self-destructive acts are perpetuated, and more violent deaths occur in *The Possessed*, than in any other major work by Dostoevsky. Most important, however, for the purpose of this investigation are the suicides of the two leading protagonists in the novel, namely, Aleksei Kirillov and Nikolai Stavrogin.

Kirillov

The suicide of Kirillov has received more critical attention than any other act of self-destruction depicted in the works of Dostoevsky. Kirillov kills himself on principle just to prove a point. His suicide is "logical". He himself explains the reasons which impel him to take his own life. In fact, we are presented in the novel with a psychological autopsy of a would-be suicide who makes no secret of his intentions and who reveals to the outside world the motives which drive him to self-destruction. In addition, Kirillov's suicide is not the private matter of an individual who decides willfully to part with his life. Within the context of the novel, Kirillov's intended actions have also become the concern of other people who are not in the least interested in his personal well-being or in saving his life. Kirillov's contemplated suicide has become closely intertwined with one of the main conflicts in the novel; he has agreed to take upon himself the responsibility for the murder of Shatov and thus cover up the criminal activities of Petr Verkhovensky and his collaborators.

Kirillov first appears in the narrative when he is introduced by Liputin to Stepan Trofimovich Verkhovensky. Liputin hastens to inform those present that Kirillov "is writing a very interesting article dealing with the causes of the increase of suicide in Russia, and, generally speaking, the causes that lead to the increase or decrease of suicide in society."[1] Kirillov is very excited and incensed when the subject of suicide is mentioned. He rejects Liputin's allegations that he is writing an article or indeed that he is publishing anything. Liputin hastens to correct himself by saying that Kirillov "is only collecting observations, and the essence of the question, or, so to say, its moral aspect he is not touching at all. And, indeed, he rejects morality itself altogether, and holds with the last new principle of general destruction for the sake of the ultimate good."[2] Kirillov, basically a reticent man, is furious with Liputin's pronouncements, the more so since the latter clearly confuses some of his notions. Thus it is made immediately evident that the problem of suicide agitates Kirillov very much, and that it touches in him a very deep personal chord.

The ideas, the nature and the role of Kirillov in the novel are disclosed in three crucial dialogues. The first conversation is with the narrator, the second with Stavrogin and the third with Petr Verkhovensky, taking place in the last moments of Kirillov's life. In his brief conversation with the narrator, Kirillov admits that Liputin is correct in alleging that he writes about suicide. Kirillov asserts that all he seeks is to investigate "the causes why men dare not to kill themselves."[3] According to Kirillov, man does not kill himself because he is afraid of pain and of God:

> "Life is pain, life is terror, and man is unhappy.... Now man loves life, because he loves pain and terror.... Life is given now for pain and terror, and that's the deception. Now man is not yet what he will be. There will be a new man, happy and proud. For whom it will be the same to live or not to live, he will be the new man. He who will conquer pain and terror will himself be a god.... God is the pain of the fear of death. He who will conquer pain and terror will become himself a god.... Everyone who wants the supreme freedom must dare to kill himself.... He who dares to kill himself is God."[4]

Kirillov adds, however, that only the man who kills himself for no other reason than to kill fear will become God.

In his discussion with Stavrogin, Kirillov expounds his ideas further. He makes clear that by killing himself he seeks to conquer death and to become a man-God. Kirillov's confrontation and exchange with Petr Verkhovensky gives the final expression of his philosophical beliefs. It exhibits distinctly the internal dichotomy of his nature. Kirillov tells Petr that "if there is no God, then I am God";[5] a statement which amazes the latter because he cannot understand how and why Kirillov would become a God. Kirillov explains that "if God exists, all is His will and from His will I cannot escape. If not, it's all my will and I am bound to show self-will.... The highest point of my self-will is to kill myself with my own hand."[6] Kirillov claims that he has "no higher idea than disbelief in God.... Man has done nothing but invent God so as to go on living, and not to kill himself.... To recognise that there is no God and not to recognise at the same instant that one is God oneself is an absurdity, else one would certainly kill oneself."[7] Thus, Kirillov says that he will kill himself to prove his independence and his terrible freedom. For Kirillov, the salvation for all consists in proving to everyone that his idea is correct.

The image of Kirillov appears relatively late in Dostoevsky's rough sketches to the novel. There is no detailed depiction of his personal character traits in the early drafts. We are told, however, that "the engineer volunteered to shoot himself for the general cause — and, what is most important: the role of the engineer is real."[8] There is no mention at this point of the engineer's philosophical notions or of the ideological reasons for his impending suicide. Structurally, the appearance of Kirillov on the pages of the novel is connected with the discussion of the subject of suicide and his final departure is marked by his actual physical self-destruction.

There are different hypotheses as to the actual prototype of Kirillov. V.I. Kel'siev suggests that Kirillov is modelled after P.I. Krasnopevtsev, an artillery officer who committed suicide.[9] L. Grossman, on the other hand, presumes that a member of the Petrashevsky circle, Konstantin Timkovsky, is the prototype for Kirillov.[10] According to A.S. Dolinin, Dostoevsky gives Kirillov the name of Tikhon Zadonsky — in the world Kirillov,[11] while V.A. Tunimanov intimates that the name Kirillov has possibly been taken from the name of N.S. Kirillov, the publisher of the *Pocket Dictionary of Foreign Words*.[12] According to another hypothesis, the beliefs of Kirillov resemble closely those of one of the members of the Nechaev circle, A.K. Malikov, who has adopted the "new Religion" according to which as soon as man believes that he possesses the qualities of God, all evil will disappear and life on earth will become paradise.[13] Dostoevsky apparently sees some resemblance between the views of Malikov and that of Kirillov because he writes down in his notebooks for 1875-76 that "I was told *that Kirillov* is not clear. I could tell you about Mal'kov (sic)."[14]

Another note in the early drafts to the novel indicates that Dostoevsky views Kirillov as a truly Russian character, that is, a man who is forever in search of truth and who is ready to suffer and sacrifice himself for a noble idea. Dostoevsky writes there that "to sacrifice oneself for the truth is a national trait of this generation. God bless him (Kirillov) and give him the understanding of the truth, because the main concern of the problem is to clarify what one is to consider the truth. This is the main aim of the novel."[15] It is suggested that Kirillov's idea of man-godhood was devised by Dostoevsky under the influence of his personal experiences of the 1840s in the Petrashevsky circle. Members of the circle were debating modern notions of religion, including those of Feuerbach. In one of his articles Petrashevsky discusses the ideas of Feuerbach on religion. He asserts that "naturalism ... is a science which unites pantheism and materialism and considers deity nothing more than a general and higher form of man's thinking. It is transformed into atheism, and finally anthropotheism, i.e., a science which recognizes man as the only highest being in nature."[16] According to V.L. Komarovich

> "Dostoevsky connects logically the suicide of Kirillov with the atheistic dogma of Feuerbach (religion, the idea of God, is rooted in the fear of weak and ignorant man). Since in the 1840s Feuerbach was close to Fourier, suicide as a means of surmounting fear, of overcoming God by the 'godly' man — is 'in the style' of the humanism of the forties — the humanism which was turning, but did not turn completely, towards atheism. Dostoevsky knew well about it, and, therefore, he stressed the transitional, vacillating condition of Kirillov; that between faith and disbelief, between man-god and Christ."[17]

A view similar to that expressed by Petrashevsky is also aired by N.A. Speshnev, another member of the Petrashevsky circle. Speshnev admits that anthropotheism, the deification of man, is a modern doctrine of the current times. Speshnev, an atheist, criticizes anthropotheism however. He claims that "anthropotheism is also a religion, only a different one. The object of deification is new, but the fact of deification remains the same. Instead of god-man we now have man-god. All that has changed is the order of the words."[18] For Speshnev, the avowed atheist, any religion is anathema. He sees little difference between the principles of god-manhood and man-godhood.

On the artistic plane according to V.V. Vinogradov, Dostoevsky's portrayal of Kirillov has been influenced by V. Hugo's "Le dernier jour d'un condamné" (The Last Day of a Man Condemned to Death). The condemned man has a dream in which he finds himself in a dark room with a little old woman. Candle in hand he tries to locate her when suddenly she bites him in the hand.[19] Similarly, Petr Verkhovensky, being in doubt as to Kirillov's final intentions, pursues the invisible Kirillov candle in hand. All of a sudden he becomes aware of a fearful pain in the little finger of his left hand and realizes he has been bitten by the bent-down form of Kirillov. Petr Verkhovensky tears his finger away and rushes headlong out of the house.[20] Vinogradov points out that the nightmarish dream of Hugo's man condemned to death is transformed by Dostoevsky into the literary reality of a pre-death frenzy by a suicide who has condemned himself to death. The motions and the actions of Hugo's mysterious old woman are passed on to Kirillov, but instead of being an expression of the condemned man's anguish, they become part and parcel of the fate of the hero who chooses to die by his own volition.[21]

Biting Petr's finger is Kirillov's last act before he finally shoots himself. It is a symbolic revenge on a man whom he despises and who forces him to commit suicide on terms previously unacceptable to him. Kirillov refuses initially to take responsibility for the crimes perpetrated by Verkhovensky. Finally, by being driven into a frenzy, he signs a note dictated to him by Verkhovensky. Instead of biting Verkhovensky's finger Kirillov could have killed his tormentor before finally putting an end to himself. Such action would be contrary to Kirillov's nature. At one point Verkhovensky suggests that instead of shooting himself, Kirillov could have killed someone else in order to demonstrate his self-will, but Kirillov retorts that "to kill some one would be the lowest point of self-will, and you show your soul in that. I am not you: I want the highest point and I'll kill myself."[22]

E. Wasiolek asserts that Petr's casual remark exposes the deception which is at the core of Kirillov's thinking. Petr shows that the low point of Kirillov's act is just as logical as the high point: "Kirillov believes that with the death of God, man will be free to be good; but the logical consequence is that without God, man will be free to do his pleasure, and neither good nor evil will exist."[23] It appears thus that in his reply to Petr Verkhovensky, Kirillov negates the freedom which he advocates; he brings back the old values from which his suicide is supposed to liberate him.

The image of Kirillov has been created by Dostoevsky under the influence of different sources and prototypes. The ideological origins of this character have greatly affected the ambivalence and duality of his nature, particularly as it relates to his attitude towards religion. Kirillov tells the narrator: "I think all my life of one thing. God has tormented me all my life."[24] It is evident that had Kirillov been either a confirmed atheist or a fervent believer, God would not have tormented him: either Kirillov would reject God altogether or he would accept God without question. But Kirillov is agonized by his internal subconscious doubts. His heart longs for faith, while his reason tells him that God is a fiction of man's imagination.

Kirillov is very much a man of this world. He is fond of children. He loves life. PetrVerkhovensky tells him that he believes perhaps "more thoroughly than any priest."[25] Kirillov counters with a story which obviously refers to the predilection of Christ. A man on a cross promises Paradise to the man next to him but neither of them finds Paradise or resurrection. Kirillov's story is reminiscent of Ippolit's argument developed under the influence of Holbein's picture of Christ's deposition from the cross. Kirillov follows the example of Ippolit when he says that "if the laws of nature did not spare even Him, have not spared even their miracle and made even Him live in a lie and die for a lie, then all the planet is a lie and rests on a lie and on mockery."[26]

Just as Holbein's picture kills Ippolit's faith, the lack of definite proof that God really exists paralyses Kirillov's inner urge and need for faith. Christ sacrifices Himself and takes upon Himself the suffering of man. According to Kirillov, Christ sacrifices Himself in vain. Because he fails to produce a miracle, He dies just like any other ordinary mortal, failing to give man the necessary proof that he is the son of God and the Saviour of man. Kirillov's reasoning anticipates Ivan Karamazov's "Legend of the Grand Inquisitor" (*Velikii inkvizitor*) in which the same argument is further developed artistically. Kirillov appears to want to imitate Christ. He also sacrifices himself out of love for man. But his sacrifice has to show man his ultimate destiny and his terrible freedom from God. Thus Kirillov usurps the place of Christ and aspires to replace Him in the universe, a fact which points, according to K. Mochulsky, to Kirillov's irrational need for God. Mochulsky suggests that "his heart cannot live without God, but his mind cannot admit the existence of God.... Kirilov kills himself not only to destroy the idea of God, but also because without God he cannot live."[27]

The character of Kirillov belongs to the great creations of Dostoevsky's art. The scene of his suicide is striking, and the ideas and theories leading to his suicide appear to be simple and logical, if not brilliant. Yet some critics suggest that the whole idea of "logical suicide" is illogical, contrary not only to human nature but also to Kirillov's character. In the view of André Gide "Kirillov's suicide is absolutely gratuitous," which means that there is in it a total "absence of outward motivation."[28] Gide goes on to assert with some justification that Kirillov's views, which are voiced in a highly pathological state of mind, are often obscure and incoherent. For Gide "we are left to unravel in it the clue to Dostoevsky's own thought,"[29] which is often as obscure ad that of Kirillov. It is also possible to question, as Irving Howe does:

> "...whether the highest expression of the will is suicide? One would suppose that a higher heroism of the will might be the choice to live.... No doubt, Dostoevsky meant to suggest here that Kirilov's ideas make him indifferent to the fate of his friends and indeed of all men, but Dostoevsky himself has shown us otherwise: he could not help presenting Kirilov as a good man. For once — it does not happen very often — Dostoevsky the novelist has been tripped up by Dostoevsky the ideologue."[30]

Irving Howe is correct in questioning Dostoevsky's basic premise. In Kirillov's theory the fear of death is allegedly to be conquered by death itself. Consequently, Kirillov's attempt to replace God-man with his own creation, man-God, leads essentially to the destruction of the very man-God he sets out to create. Howe does not enlarge on the fact that Dostoevsky defines Kirillov's ideas in extreme terms. Kirillov is a sick man and a highly enigmatic individual. He appears in the pages of the novel in a state of obsession with the idea of suicide, an idea which step by step "devours him." We do not know how Kirillov arrives at his ideas, nor do we know the reasons for his illness. V. Chizh posits that Kirillov's state of mind and his ideas are characteristic of epileptics.[31]

It is possible to suggest that in psychological terms the suicide of Kirillov should be viewed as a suicide of a sick man, a man who has become obsessed with an idea which takes control of his rational faculties. There appears to be a perverted nobility in Kirillov's dedication to his ideals and even though these ideals in themselves may seem lofty enough, the form which his devotion to his theories takes is certainly morbid.

The final scene of Kirillov's suicide is fascinating. It illustrates clearly the inner struggle between Kirillov's heart and his mind. It points to man's instinctive desire to live, an impulse which is overpowered here by his rational decision to die. Till the very last moment Verkhovensky is not sure whether Kirillov will actually shoot himself or whether Kirillov will attempt to kill him instead. Kirillov is not a man of half-measures; in the end he takes his own life.

Kirillov's suicide appears to be inspired by altruistic motives. He wants to liberate man from his fear of death and make him the master of his own destiny. But, in order to be able to kill oneself one has to be ready and willing to die. A number of psychoanalysts reject the concept of a death instinct. They claim that the human mind is incapable of conceiving death. They suggest that suicide should be viewed "as an act of self-perpetuation rather than of self-destruction, in which the individual denies the barrier separating life and death. Suicide has been seen as a paradoxical self-assertion through which man achieves a phantasied immortality. Taking one's life is an act of omnipotence because in doing so the person evades natural death."[32] This psychological explanation of suicide is amazingly close to Kirillov's theories of man-godhood, but it does not explain why and how a man altogether devoid of self-destructive instincts could kill himself.

As Alfred Alvarez states, "psycho-analysts have suggested that a man may destroy himself not because he wants to die but because there is a single aspect of himself which he cannot tolerate. A suicide of this order is a perfectionist. The flaws in his nature exacerbate him like some secret itch he cannot get at. So he acts suddenly, rashly, out of exasperation."[33] In Kirillov's case, Alvarez suggests that

> "(Kirillov) kills himself, he says, to show that he is God. But secretly he kills himself because he knows he is not God. Had his ambitions been less, perhaps he would have only attempted the deed or mutilated himself.... Compared with other revolutionaries in the novel Kirillov seems sane, tender-hearted and upright. Yet maybe his concern with godhead and metaphysical liberty consigned him, too, to the suburbs of psychosis. And this sets him apart from the majority of the inhabitants of the closed world of suicide. For them the act is neither rash nor operatic nor, in any obvious way, unbalanced. Instead it is, insidiously a vocation. Once inside the closed world, there seems never to have been

a time when one was not suicidal.... The suicide feels he has always been preparing in secret for this last act."[34]

Indeed, Kirillov is not an ordinary suicide. His suicide has been described as logical, metaphysical, pedagogical and heroic. These terms fail to give an all-embracing explanation of his personality or to take into account the whole complexity and internal conflicts of his nature.

Dostoevsky is often cited as one of the forerunners of existentialist thought. If any single thesis could be said to express most clearly the doctrine of existentialism, it would be that the possibility of choice is the central fact of human nature. Freedom of choice is the supreme good, but it can also be the greatest evil. Man is free to do anything he wants, including perpetrating acts of murder and self-destruction. Like the existentialists, Dostoevsky stresses in his art the extreme and exceptional experience of man, and his heroes express their freedom of choice in extreme terms. The underground man, and Kirillov who follows him, use their freedom to exemplify the unpredictable character of the universe they confront and to wage metaphysical rebellion against society and against themselves. By killing himself Kirillov exposes the logical implications of total freedom with terrifying clarity, because only death is the absolute proof and irrefutable argument of one's free choice. By his suicide Kirillov endorses everything Albert Camus was later to call "the absurd." But according to Camus, the absurd man accepts life while Kirillov chooses death. Therefore, Kirillov is an absurd character with one essential reservation: he refuses to accept life and he kills himself in order to assert his ultimate freedom.[35]

Stavrogin

Nikolai Vsevolodovich Stavrogin is one of Dostoevsky's most mysterious protagonists. From his very first appearance on the pages of the novel to his last act of willful self-destruction, he remains enigmatic. His actions and movements are startling, and his motives obscure. It is significant that from the very beginning of the novel Stavrogin is presented to the reader as a murderer who has escaped just punishment and has failed to repent for his crime. In the past he had participated in two duels that "had killed one of his adversaries on the spot and had maimed the other."[36] Stavrogin's past is related by the narrator who claims to have met him several years ago when the mature Stavrogin came to town for the first time.

The narrator's impressions of Stavrogin, and the latter's external appearance are described in contradictory terms. We are told that Stavrogin exhibits good sense, modesty and good manners. At the same time, he displays extraordinary physical strength, boldness and self-reliance. From the very beginning Stavrogin is introduced to us as a mysterious figure, a man whose external appearance does not reveal his inner world: "One would have thought that he must be a paragon of beauty, yet at the same time there seemed something repellent about him ... his face suggested a mask."[37] He is a man whose actions and behaviour are puzzling, inconsistent and contradictory, serving as a device to hide his real self.

Stavrogin's decorous stay in town does not last long. It is interrupted suddenly by three senseless and irrational acts. On one occasion he takes one of the respected club members, Gaganov, by the nose and leads him several steps across the room. Next, when he is invited by Liputin to a party in honour of his wife's birthday, Stavrogin unexpectedly seizes Liputin's wife around the waist and kisses her publicly on the lips with great relish, two or three times. When the governor tries to inquire from Stavrogin as to what drives him to acts which are contrary to all accepted rules, the latter, pretending that he is going to disclose a grave secret, bites the governor's ear. Stavrogin is arrested and when it is soon discovered that he suffers from acute brain fever, he is taken home to his mother, Varvara Petrovna. Several months later, upon the insistence of Varvara Petrovna, he goes abroad. It has been decided that Stavrogin's seemingly harmless, irrational pranks have been the result of a temporary illness. No one could surmise that these ostensibly minor transgressions are to cover up Stavrogin's previous major offences or that they foreshadow his future crimes. No one could suspect that Stavrogin, the great pretender and impostor, could have feigned his illness in order to avoid the wrath of the governor.

Stavrogin's personal appearance is clouded with an aura of mystery. We learn about his first stay in town from the narrator, but we are told little about his experiences before or after his arrival. Hints, allusions and insinuations help create an obscure picture of his past. We realize at once that Stavrogin exerts a mysterious power which has a peculiar effect on others. He exercises a hold on people through emotional relationships. Most people who surround him are subservient to him. He dominates everything he comes in touch with, though it might appear that he does not seek this domination and that he himself remains aloof and unmoved. The secret of Stavrogin's relationship with the four women in his life (Liza, Dasha, Mar'ia Timofeevna and Mar'ia Ignat'evna, Shatov's wife) unfolds slowly. Similarly his relationship with Shatov and with Kirillov, each of whom he has infected with ideas reflecting different sides of his own complex personality, is disclosed step by step.

Schematically Stavrogin stands on a pinnacle — strong, self-assured, and indifferent. All others try to reach out for different parts of his divided personality. They delude themselves in thinking that the one side of his dark nature to which they appeal expresses the totality of his existence. Most of them fail to understand the complexity of Stavrogin's nature or to appreciate the internal dichotomy of his character. Stavrogin appears to be passive while all others are actively in pursuit of some goal. But in this ostensible inactivity he generates corruption, destruction and death. From among those who reach out for him only Dasha and Petr Verkhovensky survive; all others perish. Although Stavrogin does not participate directly in their destruction, his indifference makes each murder and death possible, if not inevitable: Stavrogin knows that Shatov will be murdered and he does nothing to prevent it; he expects Kirillov's suicide, but he does nothing to dissuade him; his indifference and lack of concern for the welfare of those who worship him lead to the deaths of Liza, Mar'ia Ignat'evna and Mar'ia Timofeevna. Even his illegitimate child by Shatov's wife, the symbol of possible regeneration and future life for Stavrogin, is not spared; it dies before its mother's demise.

Stavrogin's detachment from life and from the living is an expression of total freedom without God. This freedom deteriorates into negation and self-will, eventually leading, for Dostoevsky, to the downfall and disintegration of those around him. Stavrogin reaches the highest level of this freedom. He is totally in control of his own actions and movements. he dominates completely all those who come in touch with him. His personality radiates terror and ruin. In the end he remains alone. Those who reached out for him are swept away by the indifference generated by his terrible freedom. In the end, the tragic, demonic figure of Stavrogin is consumed by the same fire which destroyed those who saw him as their teacher, leader, Prince or lover. As long as the world of petty intrigue and petty devils continues to exist, there is room for Stavrogin in it. But as soon as this corrupted environment is destroyed and most of Stavrogin's worshippers perish, there is no longer any justification for his existence and he must face retribution for his sins and crimes.

Stavrogin lives in a a society full of petty demons, he himself being the archdemon, the initiator and inspiration for most crimes. He is possessed by the spirit of evil which is at the same time the spirit of negation and emptiness. According to Dostoevsky, complete negation is impossible for man. The existing vacuum must be filled. Ideally this spiritual void would be filled with ardent faith. In *The Possessed* except for Shatov, who replaces the theory of negation with ardent belief, ethical voids are filled mainly by false appearances. Kirillov gives up faith and denies God by creating a new man-God. Negation leads to substitution. Petr Verkhovensky fills his void with the adoration and worship of a leader — Stavrogin. Most others fill the vacuum with illusory social, political or personal endeavours. Only Stavrogin remains empty. He is beyond the confines of good and evil; his apathy and indifference are total. He writes in his last letter to Dasha:

> "I am still capable, as I always was, of desiring to do something good, and of feeling pleasure from it; at the same time I desire evil and feel pleasure from that too. But both feelings are always too petty, and are never very strong. My desires are too weak; they are not enough to guide me.... Your brother told me that the man who loses connection with his country loses his gods, that is, all his aims.... but from me nothing has come but negation, with no greatness of soul, no force. Even negation has not come from me. Everything has always been petty and spiritless."[38]

Stavrogin is a sombre villain but he is also a tragic hero. He is very much aware of his situation. He claims that he can never lose his reason, as Kirillov does, and that he cannot deceive himself. He writes to Dasha: "I can never, never, shoot myself. I know I ought to kill myself, to brush myself off the earth like a nasty insect; but I am afraid of suicide, for I am afraid of showing greatness of soul. I know that it will be another sham again — the last deception in an endless series of deceptions. What good is there in deceiving oneself?"[39] And yet, despite this fear of suicide Stavrogin does kill himself by hanging. He does not shoot himself, for that act requires positive action often identified with the romantic, noble notion of self-sacrifice. Stavrogin is passive and indifferent to the very end. He lets the silk cord do the job. He submits passively to his fate, doing nothing to save himself, just as he does nothing to save all those who look up to him for guidance and support.

Stavrogin is portrayed as a man of great strength. he is somewhat reminiscent of Orlov in the *House of the Dead* whose power of self-control is unlimited. Yet Stavrogin also has much in common with Petrov who is ruled by reason only until he has some strong desire and then there is no obstacle on earth that can hinder him. The narrator describes Stavrogin as "one of those natures that know nothing of fear."[40] A man, as Shatov puts it, who does not "linger on the brink."[41] Stavrogin is a passive hero but he is a very decisive man. His seeming passivity is engendered by his consciousness of the meaninglessness and purposelessness of life which suppresses his motivation for positive action.

But once Stavrogin decides to act, nothing can stop him. people like Stavrogin have the inner strength and will-power to put an end to themselves. In any event, Stavrogin enters the novel as a living corpse. His soul is in a state of total narcosis. His spirit is dead. The evolution of Stavrogin's character in the novel is a progression from spiritual death to physical death. Stavrogin admits to Kirillov that the idea of suicide is not new to him. He says:

> "I sometimes have thought of it myself, and then there always came a new idea: if one did something wicked, or, worse still, something shameful, that is, disgraceful, only very shameful and ... ridiculous, such as people would remember for a thousand years and hold in scorn for a thousand years, and suddenly the thought comes: 'one blow in the temple and there would be nothing more.' One wouldn't care then for men and that they would hold one in scorn for a thousand years, would one?"[42]

The proud nature of Stavrogin could never accept personal ridicule and laughter. As he points out, suicide for him would be an escape from the judgement of men. In the final analysis his suicide is an escape and also a confession that life without meaning is an awful burden and that freedom without confines is a terrible responsibility with which even he is unable to cope. At first Stavrogin intends to flee from the boredom of Russia to Switzerland. He becomes a naturalized citizen of the canton of Uri. But he has no illusions. He is sceptical about his future there as well. He tells Dasha: "I expect nothing of Uri: I am simply going. I have not chosen a gloomy place on purpose. I have no ties in Russia — everything is alien to me there as everywhere. It's true that I dislike living there more than anywhere; but I can't hate anything even there!"[43] Stavrogin admits to Dasha his final and total bankruptcy. His intended trip to Uri, as everything else, is purposeless. He realizes that his perverted sense of values makes no distinction between love and hate or good and evil.

More importantly, according to Dostoevsky, is the fact that Stavrogin is doomed to destruction because he is a rootless creature. He has no ties with his native soil; he fails to identify with the Russian people. It is paradoxical that Stavrogin, who sows the seeds of ardent belief and of Russian nationalism in Shatov and who asserts unequivocally that "an atheist at once ceases to be a Russian," and "a man who is not orthodox could not be a Russian,"[44] is himself an atheist with no attachment to his native Russian land or to the Russian God. To Dostoevsky such an attachment could have saved Stavrogin from spiritual and physical disintegration. As K. Mochulsky suggests, Stavrogin "acknowledges the existence of God and the necessity of religion intellectually, but his heart is not with God but with the devil."[45] Stavrogin realizes that the trip to Uri would be a further self-deception and he resorts, therefore, to a final escape from which there is no return.

The character of Stavrogin has been carried over into *The Possessed* from

The Life of a Great Sinner, a major work planned by Dostoevsky. The predecessor of Stavrogin in the early drafts of *The Possessed* is the nameless Prince. The Prince has many personal traits characteristic of Stavrogin, although in the beginning he is still redeemable. Dostoevsky's plans for the character of the Prince change many times. His final destiny alternates between suicide and regeneration. At one point we read in the drafts, that the Prince submits without reservations to the views and influence of the Old Believer Golubov who has been converted to the Orthodox faith. Golubov maintains that the essence of life is "humility and self-control, and that God and the kingdom of heaven are within us, in our self-control, and our freedom is there as well."[46] On the next page, however, the Prince shoots himself because he cannot accept the fact that he lacks attachment to the soil.[47] Then again, the Prince is a real Russian; he prays ardently and he "surprises even his mother by this wild energy of his new convictions."[48] The Prince makes a declaration of love to the "pupil" — the future Dasha — and then, all of a sudden, shoots himself.

The character of the Prince evolves step by step, finally assuming the image of Stavrogin in the novel; however, the idea of the main hero's self-destruction is ever present. In the beginning he shoots himself for no apparent reason; it is even presumed that he is insane. In another version he goes to Uri and hangs himself there.[49] In the final version of the novel, Stavrogin does not go to Uri. He hangs himself in his mother's house on Russian soil, leaving a short note: "No one is to blame. I did it myself."

The image of Stavrogin in *The Possessed* has been greatly affected by the different stages of development of his predecessor in *The Life*. This dependence accounts to a degree for his mysterious essence. It would be difficult to ascertain whether Stavrogin has been intentionally created as an enigmatic hero in order to enhance the elements of intrigue and suspense in the novel or whether one should consider his contradictory image as a shortcoming connected with the artistic evolution of a character carried over into the novel from a different literary plan.

Initially Dostoevsky intended to incorporate into the novel a chapter entitled "At Tikhon's" which would contain Stavrogin's confession. The deleted chapter was to follow the chapter "Ivan the Tsarevich" in which Petr Verkhovensky expresses his adoration for Stavrogin and reveals the political plans he has for him. Despite the changes introduced by Dostoevsky in order to tone down the meaning of the confession, the editor of *The Russian Herald* (*Ruskii vestnik*), Katkov, refused to publish the chapter in the original serial publication of the novel. Later, though still in Dostoevsky's lifetime, when the novel was republished in book form, the author did not resort to the inclusion of the banned chapter, choosing rather to retain the novel in its original form.

The shadow of the omitted chapter continues to hover over the critical discussion of *The Possessed*. There is as yet no unanimity on the relationship of the confession to the canonical text of the novel. R. Peace, for example, suggests that "its exclusion not only disturbs the balance of the novel, it also witholds essential information about Stavrogin."[50] E. Wasiolek, on the other hand, asserts that "the Stavrogin that appears in the expurgated confession chapter is unnecessary.... There is no inconsistency between this chapter and the Stavrogin that appears in the novel, as some critics have claimed. Those who see a repentant Stavrogin in his visit to Tikhon fail once again to understand the dialectical nature of Dostoevsky's world, for Stavrogin's 'confession' is but another test of his strength. The portrait of Stavrogin in the confession chapter is morally consistent, but dramatically inconsistent."[51] Similarly, Iu. Kudriavtsev propounds an idea that Stavrogin's confession would have ruined the whole novel by destroying the image of its main hero, because "Stavrogin, an extremely enigmatic individual ... could have been turned into an ordinary criminal";[52] a simple murderer.

One has to bear in mind that had Dostoevsky been permitted to include the chapter "At Tikhon's" in the serial publication of the novel, the future development of the plot could have been considerably different to what we have now. It is well known that Stavrogin has come into *The Possessed* from the drafts of *The Life of a Great Sinner* where the initial idea is to have the hero regenerate. Thus, the possibility of Stavrogin's redemption would have made his suicide unnecessary and would have led the development of his character along the path envisioned by Dostoevsky for Raskolnikov. The inclusion of the confession in the novel would have changed the whole emphasis in the narrative. Without the confession, Stavrogin's greatest crime is the fate of all those who depend on his theories, ideas and emotions, but are forsaken and driven to destruction by his indifference. With the confession, Stavrogin's greatest crime is the abuse of Matresha which leads to her suicide, an act which, in this case, is tanatamount to murder and which could certainly have been prevented.

The confession expresses, better than anything else in the novel, the internal dichotomy of Stavrogin's personality. He comes to Tikhon because of a great fear. He is confronted by a devil — an hallucination which is the reflection of his troubled conscience. he appears to suffer from a sense of guilt which is, however, mocking and spiteful. The hallucination is the embodiment of Stavrogin's attitude towards others and the fear of what he sees in himself. It reflects an inherent need of man for sympathy, for some kind of love and for a sense of comradeship. Despite this positive impulse Stavrogin's confession comes from pride, rather than from humility. Stavrogin wants Tikhon to forgive him; he does not care about others. In reality he does not even want forgiveness, but rather defiance. His name — Stavrogin — which embodies the double meaning of "cross bearer" and "horn", reflects his behaviour. He pretends to be ready to take upon himself the "cross" but shows his horns instead.

Had the confession been included in the novel there would be a hint that, subconsciously at least, Stavrogin is able to expiate and to confess. It would mean that in spite of everything Stavrogin makes an attempt to make life more bearable. It would show that he is capable of turning for outside help. In this sense the confession at Tikhon's is similar to Stavrogin's letter to Dasha in which he asks her to help him save himself from himself. Paradoxically, Stavrogin does not realize that even though he is capable of asking for help, he is too proud and scornful to be able to accept help from others. This pride prevents him from accepting Tikhon's offer or waiting for Dasha's reply to his letter before he commits suicide.

R. Peace suggests that since the details of Stavrogin's suicide "reproduce those of another suicide, that of Matresha.... Stavrogin's suicide may be interpreted as an act of oblique contrition for her death."[53] It is necessary to note, however, that the details are external only, because the causes of these suicides are completely different. Matresha's suicide is the desperate act of a young child whose heart and conscience have been outraged and savagely wounded. It is an act of passive rebellion against the social forces which fail to respect and protect those who are too young to take care of themselves. Matresha is a child; her faith and moral values are still uncorrupted. She realizes that she has committed a grave sin, and in her delirium she repeats "I killed God."[54] She is in despair because her childish world has crumbled. She is too young and inexperienced to adapt to her new position as a woman in society, nor can she go on living as she lived before. Dostoevsky's concern for the well-being of young children is well known. In *The Diary of a Writer* he expresses his outrage for the numerous incidents of child abuse in real life. In his fiction children often symbolize hope, purity, innocence, trust and beauty. In *Crime and Punishment* Dostoevsky amplifies Svidrigailov's corrupted nature by including among his victims several children, one of whom has been cruelly abused and driven to suicide by hanging herself in a fashion similar to that of Matresha's.

Furthermore, Stavrogin's suicide can be interpreted as an act of penitence for Matresha's death only if his confession had become part of the novel. But since Dostoevsky chose not to incorporate the banned chapter into the book version of *The Possessed* and since Matresha's name is not even mentioned there, we have little reason to connect the suicides of Matresha and Stavrogin. It has been pointed out already that had Stavrogin been able to express real remorse and penitence for his deeds, there would be no need for him to commit suicide. E.H. Carr asserts that most characters in *The Possessed* are "more or less convincingly portrayed, from the real world; Stavrogin and Kirillov are pure fictions of the imagination, and their inspiration is literary and philosophical rather than historical."[55]

In his discussion of the character of Stavrogin, Sergei Bobrov makes an interesting observation. He says that "the illusory strength of Dostoevsky's evil heroes is expressed in the fact that they appear to us in a state of total disintegration and that, in general, they represent a category 'of people who did not manage yet to shoot themselves in their leisure time'."[56] These people have little to contribute *to* life and need nothing *from* life. They are people who are bored, disenchanted and tired of life, not because they work hard, but because they have never done anything useful for man and society. According to Bobrov, such life leads to moral corruption and spiritual disintegration which are logical steps before final physical annihilation.

Stavrogin's suicide may surprise and shock the reader, but Dostoevsky takes great pains to prepare for it adequately. Early in the novel Stavrogin admits to Kirillov that sometimes he thinks about suicide. The fact that shortly before destroying himself Stavrogin states explicitly in his letter to Dasha that he has no intention of killing himself, is also an oblique indication that he is preoccupied with the notion of suicide. Stavrogin commits suicide only after all the positive elements connected with his personality, and expressed in those around him, are destroyed. Yuri Glazov suggests that Shatov was the only force which could help him survive: "Even his murderous slap could be considered as a final attempt to revive Stavrogin."[57] But Stavrogin does not prevent the murder of Shatov so his own destruction becomes inescapable.

Stavrogin's suicide is an act which reflects his creator's Weltanschauung. According to Dostoevsky, a Russian who loses his roots in the Russian soil and his faith in the Russian God, is doomed to destruction. Stavrogin's suicide is also an ethical symbol. It signifies the impossibility of living in a moral vacuum. It symbolizes the absurdity of absolute demonic freedom which leads to the disintegration of the personality. His suicide is an act of defiance which expresses the hero's cosmic despair, his tragic negation of life and his inability to surmount the internal dichotomy of his nature.

Another suicide in the novel is a nineteen year old boy. He is a nameless youth whose fate has no connection with the main plot of the narrative whatsoever. We are told by the narrator in an account resembling a newspaper report, that in a nearby hotel a boy shot himself straight in the heart, leaving a note that "no one was to blame for his death, that he had killed himself because he had 'squandered' four hundred roubles."[58] The boy was given his family's life savings and was sent to town by his widowed mother to buy a trousseau for his eldest sister. Instead, he got drunk, went to visit the gypsy camp, wasted all his money and killed himself. That is all we are told about the suicide or about the circumstances of his death. Little is known about his background or about his past. There is no way that we could ascertain the real motives which determined his actions. But that is not what is important to Dostoevsky. The writer uses this little episode in the life of the ill-fated boy in order to expose the corrupted and philistine nature of all the "petty demons" who come to view the dead body of the unfortunate youth. For them the misfortune of others is a happy diversion. Liza, Mavrikii Nikolaevich, Petr Verkhovensky, Nikolai Stavrogin and those accompanying them, are on their way to visit the saint and prophet, Semen Iakovlevich. When they stop to view the suicide they do not show feeling, compassion or concern for the fate of the dead boy or his family. They "stared at him with greedy curiosity. In every misfortune of one's neighbour there is always something cheering for an onlooker — whoever he may be."[59]

The opinions expressed by the visitors are cold, detached, even heartless: "One observed that his was the best way out of it ... another observed that he had had a good time if only for a moment."[60] Most important for the logical sequence of the novel is the opinion expressed by a third observer who "suddenly blurted out the inquiry why people had begun hanging and shooting themselves among us of late, as though they had suddenly lost their roots, as though the ground were giving way under every one's feet."[61] We have no evidence that the boy kills himself because he has lost his roots. Although we do not know Stavrogin's reaction to the remarks of the observer, these casual comments point to the dead spirit of Stavrogin and to his impending suicide for reasons similar to those expressed by the dispassionate observer.

The suicide of the nameless boy in *The Possessed* is similar to the suicide of the nameless clerk in "The Eternal Husband." Both are events which have little connection with the main plots of the narratives, however, in both cases the suicides reflect upon the fates and actions of leading protagonists. In "The Eternal Husband" the suicide of the clerk triggers a chain of events which leads to the death of Liza. In *The Possessed* the suicide of the boy reflects upon the corrupted nature of Stavrogin who "squanders" all his spiritual and ethical resources which are indispensable to the sustenance of one's life.

Dostoevsky portrays suicide in *The Possessed* either as a psychologically convincing fact of life or as an ethical symbol and an expression of his own world-outlook. The suicide or suicidal intent of secondary and minor characters serve as an artistic device in the novel. He also makes use of certain suicides which may have little relevance to the main events in the novel, to heighten the elements of suspense and intrigue. For example, at the conclusion of the novel it is reported that after the crimes of Petr Verkhovensky and his group have been discovered, one of its members (Liamshin) makes an unsuccessful attempt to commit suicide after which he runs to the authorities and confesses everything.[62] In the early drafts of *The Possessed* even Shatov's wife makes an attempt to kill herself. She "drowns herself, but she is pulled out and dies later."[63]

5. A RAW YOUTH (PODROSTOK, 1875)

A Raw Youth can be regarded as a minor novel of the mature Dostoevsky. It lacks the unity of plot and the intensity of narration characteristic of Dostoevsky's mature works. What started out as a narrative about children, develops into a novel about the relationship of a father and his illegitimate son. *A Raw Youth* is a combination of old themes and artistic devices used by Dostoevsky in his previous works and developed further in *The Brothers Karamazov*. Artistic perfection is often sacrificed in the novel for the purpose of creating suspense and an air of mystery in order to enhance the readers' interest in the narrative. *A Raw Youth* is the only novel by the mature Dostoevsky which does not culminate in violent death or in which the development of the plot is not triggered by a murder occurring in the beginning of the narrative. The novel incorporates, however, more than its share of actual, attempted and contemplated suicides. Most of these are peripheral to the main plot and, perhaps for this reason, not always adequately substantiated, psychologically.

Kraft

The suicide of the Russified German, Kraft, is often compared with the "logical" suicide of Kirillov. Indeed, both arrive at the decision of killing themselves through a logical deduction from a certain idea but both the motives and ideas driving them in their actions are different. Kirillov's objective is to save mankind through self-sacrifice. His suicide is to show man that he who has conquered the fear of death, has also conquered God. Kraft does not entertain such elevated ideas. He does not pretend to sacrifice himself for anyone. He is an unassuming, mild and delicate young man of twenty-six whose suicide is a passive expression of protest against the existing order of things. His suicide is a confession that he is helpless to do anything to change the situation which he reviles.

Kraft is overwhelmed by the notion that the Russians are "a second rate people destined to serve as the raw material for a nobler race, and not to play an independent part in the history of humanity."[1] He assumes that since his idea will result in the future paralysis of the activity of every Russian, then the Russian people are doomed to destruction and, therefore, life is meaningless and not worth living. This assumption drives him to despair.

The only thing in common between Kirillov and Kraft is on a psychological plane in that both are obsessed by ideas which influence and determine their violent self-destructive acts. Vasin, an acquaintance of Kraft, suggests "that Kraft's conclusion is not a mere logical theory but, so to say, a theory that has been transmuted into a feeling. All natures are not alike; in some man a logical deduction is sometimes transmuted into a very powerful emotion which takes possession of the whole being, and is sometimes very difficult to dislodge or to alter. To cure such a man the feeling itself must be changed, which is only possible by replacing it by another, equally powerful one. That's always difficult, and in many cases impossible."[2] It follows that ideas, values or principles which concern people are slowly transmuted into emotions and feelings which subsequently take hold and dominate the rational level of man's consciousness without him even being aware of it. According to Vasin's interpretation, both Kirillov and Kraft only appear to be in control of their rational faculties; in reality they are victims of their own emotions and feelings which are influenced and shaped by their ideas.

Kraft, who is connected with the Dergachev circle of revolutionary conspirators, has arrived at his ideas on the basis of his analysis of current Russian society. According to him society is dominated by a pervasive materialism and lack of spirituality. Kraft claims that "the present day is the golden age of mediocrity and callousness, of passion for ignorance, idleness, inefficiency, a craving for everything ready-made. No one thinks; it's rare for anyone to work out an idea for himself."[3] It is apparent that Kraft excludes himself from this generalization. He separates himself from the masses by working out a theory which repudiates the existing situation. His idea is a negative one; it defines the present situation but it neither sets forth any clear, positive objective for the future, nor specifies how the present situation could be changed for the better. Kraft's idea, which decries the meaninglessness of his life, does not fill his spiritual vacuum but rather creates a new, more dangerous void which leads to his downfall.

Kraft's ideas are not in tune with the ideas of other members of the Dergachev circle. One of them, Tikhomirov, argues, for example, that man has to rid himself of national prejudices and work for the welfare of humanity in general without making a distinction between different races. Kraft, however, is unconvinced. He admits that he cannot "understand how, if one is under the influence of some over-mastering idea which completely dominates one's mind and one's heart, one can live for something else which is outside that idea."[4]

Kraft's vision for Russia's future destiny has antithetical parallels with the vision that Shatov expresses in *The Possessed.* On the surface their ideas appear to be similar, but in essence they are very different. Shatov's faith in the future of Russia is limitless. Kraft, on the other hand, is subconsciously aware of his foreign extraction. He perceives that his own rootlessness makes him unable, despite his fervent desire, to identify completely with the Russian people. It is possible to surmise that Kraft hates in others what he sees and dislikes in himself. It is paradoxical that Kraft kills himself not because he opposes the ideals of someone like Shatov. On the contrary, one suspects that he commits suicide because he cannot become a Shatov. That is, he cannot become consumed by the flame of irrational faith in the Russian God and in the Russian people. Kraft's emotions and feelings are the result of a logical deduction from an idea which does not provide for the very possibility of achieving the desired goal.

Kraft is a character brought into the novel from real life. According to the memoirs of A.F. Koni (a public prosecutor in the city of Kazan in the early 1870s), a young man named Kramer who has been a student of Professor B.N. Chicherin at Moscow University, committed suicide in a manner and for reasons strikingly similar to those of Kraft. I.I. Lapshin points out that although the character of Kraft is not a naturalistic copy of any living model, there are so many similarities between the fates of Kraft and Kramer that there could be no doubt whatsoever that Kramer is the prototype and real model for the image of Kraft.[5] Both Kramer and Kraft are obsessed with similar ideas, and Kramer's assertion that "the Russian people have already fulfilled all that has been preordained for them by Providence, and they have no historical future and are destined only to serve as manure for younger nations which will, probably, come from the East"[6] is strikingly reminiscent of Kraft's pronouncements. Both Kramer and Kraft have German sounding names. Both shoot themselves: Kramer at noon and Kraft in the evening. Both begin to write diaries before their death: Kramer one week before his suicide and Kraft three days before his death. Both show concern for the appearance of their bodies after death. They feel chilly before shooting themselves; Kramer wants a drink of cognac, Kraft wants a glass of wine to warm himself up and both give up the idea because drinking might cause an increase in the flow of blood.

It is possible to surmise that the self-destruction of Kraft, as well as the other suicides depicted in *A Raw Youth*, have been prompted by, and in turn reflect, the times in which the novel has been written. In the early 1870s suicide reached epidemic proportions in Russian cities. It was widely discussed on the pages of the periodical press. Representatives of different ideological and political circles sought different explanations for this pervading phenomenon. Leftists and radicals approached suicide as a social problem primarily blaming difficult economic conditions for the ever-growing increase in the rate of suicide in major Russian cities. Conservative writers, on the other hand, acknowledged the social essence of the problem but they also sought different explanations for the high suicide rate in Russia.

Prince V.P. Meshchersky, for example, equates suicide with nihilism, and he makes an attempt to explain the increase in the suicide rate among young people by the growth of nihilism.[7] Meshchersky decries the fact that the suicide of young people endangers the very existence of the nation. He also claims that contemporary literature only "depicts suicides, but it says nothing about the spiritual aspect of this terrible phenomenon."[8] Dostoevsky seems to differ somewhat with the views of Meshchersky. In the early drafts of *A Raw Youth*, the future Versilov expresses an opinion that "in essence we were the real nihilists — the eternal seekers of a higher ideal. Now is the turn of indifferent blockheads or monks. The former are business-like who, by the way, despite their efficiency, often shoot themselves. The monks are socialists; their faith is as deep as madness and they never shoot themselves."[9] According to this character, real nihilism is based on socialism and since the faith of socialists and their dedication to their ideals are profound to distraction, there is no need for them to commit suicide. Only those who have become nihilists by mistake can kill themselves.[10]

In another place in the early drafts, Vasin the Minor and the future Versilov discuss the problem of suicide. Many reasons for self-destruction are advanced. It is claimed that although some kill themselves out of egotism or vanity it is the lack of a guiding ideal in life and the disappearance of the guiding thread and connections which hold a people back from desperate actions, which are cited as the main reasons for the increase in the number of suicides.[11] An opinion is expressed, in this discussion, that the old order of things has been destroyed. It was, perhaps, a bad order but it was better than no order at all. Now there is total disorder and confusion. Man exists in a total void, in a situation which often leads to self-destruction. Most important is the fact that all suicides "search for something; they ask questions to which they can find no answers. They are interested in something beyond their personal concerns."[12] They are unable to fulfil their lofty aspirations or find satisfaction in their endeavours. Thus, Kraft can be regarded as one of the misguided young men who have lost their path in a complicated and contradictory world. He is one of those people who cannot find within themselves the strength necessary to overcome the complexities of their age.

Kraft executes his suicidal designs with mathematical precision. He retains his consciousness till the very last moment of his life. He sits in a dark room because he does not want to light a candle for fear that it might set fire to something when he is dead. The last moments of his life are witness to his strength of will and awareness. Yet Vasin observes evasively about Kraft's suicide that "it was clear that he assumed stupidity and weakness of intellect."[13] Vasin's statement symbolizes the extreme irony of human fate because the ultimate wisdom of man's existence is expressed in his ability to affirm and cope with life, rather than submit to the dark forces of self-destruction. Kraft is strong enough to die in a dignified manner, but he is too weak to live in a world in which the struggle between evil and goodness is the order of the day.

It might appear from the preceding discussion that the image of Kraft has been created and developed with the sole purpose of being an ideational symbol similar to that of Kirillov. The character of Kraft is indeed a reflection of the social and spiritual phenomena of the day, but his role in the novel and his suicide are not limited to ideological or symbolic dimensions only. The plot of the novel is moved and complicated by two mysterious letters. One letter is by a certain Stolbeev, whose will gives rise to Versilov's lawsuit with the Prince Sokolsky. In this letter, written before his death, Stolbeev sets forth his wishes and he expresses them in favour of the Sokolskys. The other letter is by Katerina Nikolaevna Akhmakov who is loved by both father and son, Versilov and Arkadii. Katerina Nikolaevna's husband's gambling habits have left her at his death without a farthing. She inquires in this letter whether her wealthy old father could be declared incompetent to manage his own affairs and legally be put under her guardianship. Both letters were in the hands of the recently deceased Moscow lawyer Andronikov.

Before his death Andronikov gave the letters to his favourite niece, Mar'ia Ivanovna (the wife of Arkadii's former tutor, Nikolai Semenovich, with whom Arkadii boarded for many years in the same grammar school in Moscow). The first letter was in the hands of Kraft who had been a paid assistant to Andronikov. Mar'ia Ivanovna instructed Kraft, in accordance with the wishes of her deceased uncle, to hand the letter over to Arkadii. The letter of Katerina Nikolaevna was in the possession of Arkadii. He received it directly from Mar'ia Ivanovna before his departure from Moscow. But even Kraft did not know who had the letter and he suspected that it was in the hands of Versilov. Were Kraft to remain alive, however, he certainly could have found out the whereabouts of the letter in question.

Andronikov, Mar'ia Ivanovna and her husband do not appear in the novel directly. We learn about them from secondary sources with Kraft as the link connecting them with the main plot. It is a link which at a certain point becomes redundant. With Kraft alive the mystery of the letters, on which much of the intrigue in the novel hinges, can easily be solved. With Kraft dead, however, the mystery of the letters becomes almost impossible to disentangle. The letter of Katerina Akhmakov is, to a great extent, the mainspring of the action in the novel. Both father and son try to use this letter to blackmail the woman they love. Similarly, the subplot, in which Arkadii is involved with the scoundrel Lambert, is moved by the latter's desire to also use this letter in order to extort money from Mrs. Akhmakov. In fact, Katerina Nikolaevna does try to recover the mysterious letter. She even approaches Mar'ia Ivanovna with her request, but is advised to see Kraft in Petersburg. Katerina Nikolaevna does go to see Kraft, but all she can find out is that he shot himself the day before. Kraft's role in the novel has been completed. His death makes it impossible for Katerina Nikolaevna to unravel the secret of the letter, and the main plot can now develop further along the path envisioned by the author.

It appears thus that the image of Kraft plays a double role in the novel. Firstly, Kraft helps set in motion much of the external intrigue. Secondly, having fulfilled this role, Kraft is not removed from the scene with the help of some melodramatic device but rather Dostoevsky connects him with the Dergachev circle and has him commit a "logical" suicide in a manner and for reasons which are symbolic as well as characteristic of the young generation of his day.

Olia

Olia is the only mature woman who is successful in taking her own life in all of Dostoevsky's major novels. The other female characters in the novels who commit suicide are abused young girls driven to self-destruction by despair. Olia's appearance in *A Raw Youth* is brief and her role is peripheral to the main conflict. Her experiences, however, are a reflection of the social conditions in nineteenth century Russia, the moral fibre of the Russian merchant and middle class and the intricate relationships between different individuals which cannot be understood or fathomed by unenlightened outsiders. In addition, Olia's predicament helps to shed light on the enigmatic character of Vasin's stepfather, Stebelkov; she assists in exposing Stebelkov's insinuations that Versilov is the father of a baby by Lidiia Akhmakov, the dead step-daughter of Katerina Nikolaevna.

Olia is a proud, sensitive and innocent woman of about twenty. She arrives with her mother in Petersburg in a futile attempt to retrieve her deceased father's lost fortune, invested there with an unscrupulous merchant. Olia is crushed by her instant poverty and shocked by the actions of the people she encounters. She is willing to sell her labours for a crust of bread. She places an advertisement in the local paper offering lessons in all subjects. But those who respond to her advertisement are really looking to buy her body and her virtue. First a merchant offers to purchase Olia's favours and later a lady from a house of ill-repute tries to entice Olia into her services. Olia's proud nature cannot bear such indignities. She becomes delirious, raving and demanding justice.

When Versilov agrees to assist Olia and her mother, his offer of help is graciously accepted. The two women agree to borrow some money from him. It does not take long, however, for Olia to change her mind. She suspects Versilov of indecent intentions. Her previous experiences in Petersburg have shattered her faith in men. She cannot believe that anyone would choose to help her without having ulterior motives. The rumour, spread by Stebelkov, that Versilov is the father of a baby by a young girl, deeply touches her sensitive soul. She immediately sees herself in the role of that unfortunate girl. She interprets Versilov's benevolence as a cunning trick aimed at her innocence and good name. She says that the merchant who tried to buy her, insulted her "like a coarse peasant, but he (Versilov) like a cunning Jesuit."[14] She goes to Versilov's home, flings the sixty rubles in his face and abuses him in the presence of Arkadii and his mother. The next night Olia hangs herself.

Olia is one in a long line of Dostoevsky's abused, mistreated and insulted women, but she is also different than most others in a way. She is a cross between Dostoevsky's passive, innocent and abused woman, and the proud, defiant, infernal female. Olia is bitter; she values her dignity highly. She scorns pity and charity and she demands justice. When she fails to find a solution to her problems she decides in a moment of despair to take her own life. Regrettably Olia does not realize that she is the only succour to her mother and that without her, her mother's destiny will be even more difficult. Olia is not a Sonia Marmeladov; she could not sacrifice herself for the sake of others. She is incapable of true Christian submission and of accepting suffering. For that, deep faith is required, something which Olia apparently lacks.

In the language of Emile Durkheim, Olia's self-destruction can be viewed as an anomic suicide. According to Durkheim, anomic suicide "results from lack of regulation of the individual by society,"[15] and includes situations when sudden wealth or unexpected poverty leads to violent self-destruction. It is a social disease, which Durkheim claims, can and should be cured by social means. Olia arrives in the capital to face a mode of life totally different from that to which she has been accustomed. She confronts a world which is different from the idealized picture of reality described in school text-books. Her preconceived notions of a rosy future crumble before her eyes. The values instilled in her at school seem to be meaningless in the callous world of the big city. When their money runs out, Olia and her mother are faced with ever increasing poverty. In the end she resorts to the final act of desperation: suicide.

It appears that Olia's self-destruction can be defined as an anomic suicide only with certain reservations. Based on the psychological dimensions assigned to her by Dostoevsky it is questionable whether her personal problems could be cured with the help of social means. Olia's suicide is prompted by a combination of both social and personal causes. Had the make up of her personality been different, she could certainly have overcome and coped with most of her problems. Her suicide, therefore, can be viewed as a social problem on the surface only. In essence it is the result of Olia's contradictory, undisciplined and self-centred nature which fails to deal adequately with a combination of unexpected and extreme occurrences which irritate and aggravate her sensitive ego.

Before her suicide Olia writes a note to her mother which might dismay the serious reader by its frivolous tone. It reads: "Mother darling, forgive me for cutting short my début into life. Your Olya is causing you such grief."[16] Arkadii is amazed by the humorous tone of the note. He wonders how one could use such expressions at such a serious moment in life. But Versilov sees no humour in the note. He says that "the expression, of course, is inappropriate, and quite incongruous, and may ... have been picked up from some high-school slang or from some journalistic stuff; but the dead girl used it in that awful letter quite simply and earnestly."[17] Commenting on the insignificance of Kraft's last remarks in his diary, Vasin observes in his conversation with Arkadii, that the last thoughts of a suicide are sometimes extremely trivial. He says that "one such suicide complained, in fact, in a similar diary, that not one lofty idea visited him at that important hour, nothing but futile and petty thoughts."[18]

The other two suicides described in the novel, do not relate directly to the events depicted in the narrative. They are connected with one of the numerous subplots associated with the personality of Makar Ivanovich Dolgoruky. Because Makar Ivanovich embodies Dostoevsky's religious and ethical ideals in the novel, it is worthwhile exploring the meaning of these stories. Makar Ivanovich, the legal husband of Arkadii's mother and Versilov's unofficial wife, is some thirty years older than his wife. He has become a pilgrim who comes "home" once every three years. We get a closer look at him and learn about his ideas on what turns out to be, his last visit "home."

Makar Ivanovich is fond of telling stories. The two stories which Arkadii remembers and records in his biographical narrative are allegedly taken from real life. Both stories have deep religious significance and paradoxically, both culminate in what is considered to be a great sin, suicide. In one story, Makar Ivanovich tells of a retired soldier who returns to his native village, robs someone there and is put on trial. The soldier confesses to his guilt with tears and penitence but the jury finds him not guilty and sets him free. The soldier seeks his cross; he is prepared to suffer for his crime and sin. He wants to expiate his guilt. Since he is not punished by the court, he then begins to inflict self-punishment. He sinks into a fit of brooding, gives up eating and drinking and, on the fifth day, he finally hangs himself. "That's what it is to live with sin on the soul,"[19] concludes Makar Ivanovich.

The other story is about a wicked childless widower, a merchant who spends much of his time torturing and abusing all those who come in contact with him. Finally, the merchant's conscience begins to trouble him. He wants to make amends with those he has offended. He takes special care of the only surviving boy of a destitute widow whose other children have perished through his vicious actions. The boy himself had almost been thrashed to death by the merchant's men. To recompense the widow and the boy for the evil done to them, the merchant takes the boy into his house. He dresses him like a gentleman. He hires a good teacher for him. In short, he befriends the boy. But the boy remains frightened of his benefactor and continues to tremble all over at the very sight of the merchant. Finally, the boy accidentally smashes an expensive lamp and when the merchant chases after him in anger, the boy screams and runs to a nearby river. He "pressed his little fists against his breasts, looked up at the sky ... and leapt into the water... The river was rapid, and when they got him out the little thing was dead."[20] The merchant grieves sorrowfully. He entreats the boy's mother to marry him. She finally gives in and bears him a son, but the new-born baby falls ill and soon dies. The merchant realizes that his transgressions are so numerous and his sins so great that all the good he tries to do is not enough to expiate his guilt and save his soul. The repenting merchant then turns into a pilgrim hoping that for the woes and wanderings that lie before him, God will not leave him without requital.

Arkadii Dolgoruky is surprised that Makar Ivanovich delivers his religious message by telling stories which conclude in suicide, and he asks the old man for his view "upon the sin of suicide." Makar Ivanovich replies that "suicide is the greatest human sin ... but God alone is judge of it, for He alone knows all, every limit, every measure. We must pray without ceasing for such sinners."[21] Though it is evident that Makar Ivanovich does not condone suicide, it is also clear that he feels compassion and sympathy towards those who commit this great sin. He refuses to judge them. He leaves their fate to the higher justice of Providence.

Symbolically, the predicament of the soldier who refuses to live with his sin can be said to represent Makar's total selflessness, his lack of concern for his own physical and material well-being and a deep regard for his spiritual state. The soldier has been set free by the judges but he is unable to forgive himself. The verdict upsets the soldier's sense of values and his understanding of good and evil. Until now he has believed that crime and sin can be expiated only by suffering, but his new experience in the court teaches him that one can transgress and no punishment or suffering are required to atone for ones deeds. The soldier can, perhaps, accept forgiveness for his crime but in his view, it is not the prerogative of ordinary man to forgive sin. He wants to earn his absolution by expiating his guilt, however, he is adamant not to accept pardon without paying the price.

The treatment of defenseless children is often used by Dostoevsky as a device to test the ethical maturity and responsibility of adults. Makar Ivanovich here apparently expresses the author's view and does not castigate the little boy for his suicide. In any event, the boy is too young to be responsible for his actions. The suicide of the boy reflects the viciousness and depravity of the merchant. He is the cause of the child's death — he is responsible for the great sin of suicide. To Makar the door remains open for the regeneration of the sinner if he is prepared to atone for his sins, to accept suffering in a measure which is commensurate with his evil deeds. Makar's philosophy of life is deeply optimistic: there is hope in this world for everyone. The road to spiritual salvation is through selfless and compassionate service to mankind and to God.

The artistic composition and structure of *A Raw Youth* rely heavily on the use of melodramatic devices and artistic contrivances such as mystery, intrigue, surprise and suspense. The ominous letter, which could decide the fate of Katerina Nikolaevna's inheritance, creates much of the suspense in the novel. The melodramatic conclusion in which Katerina Nikolaevna is confronted by Versilov, Arkadii and Lambert, each of them having his own designs on her person, is the final surprise in the novel. Versilov disarms Lambert, attempts to shoot Katerina Nikolaevna and finally is wounded when he attempts to kill himself. The hero of this confrontation is, of course, Arkadii, the narrator. He saves Katerina by deflecting Versilov's aim. Then he saves Versilov by thwarting his suicidal intentions. The only explanation given by the narrator for Versilov's attempted self-destruction is that "in one instant he had lost his reason," and that "this was a man utterly beside himself."[22] It is quite possible that the usually composed Versilov could have lost his self-control at the sight of Lambert threatening Katerina with a gun. It is difficult, however, to believe that Versilov's largely concealed morbid passion for Katerina Nikolaevna could generate such an upsurge of emotions and loss of self-control that he would attempt, first to kill her, and then to shoot himself. We are made aware in the course of the novel of Versilov's inner duality; we know that he is an enigmatic character whose actions are often puzzling and obscure. yet, there is little in the novel that could psychologically substantiate Versilov's attempted suicide.

In several of the early drafts of the novel, Dostoevsky has the future Versilov commit suicide,[23] but with further development of the plot the author later abandons this idea. The early drafts differ considerably from the final version. In the earliest drafts the future Versilov meets a woman with a daughter, Liza. In several versions Versilov seduces Liza and she hangs herself.[24] In another version she shoots herself.[25] K. Mochulsky suggests that the early Liza is the future Olia in the novel.[26] In one of the following drafts, the Minor and Liza have an eight year old sickly brother; all three are illegitimate children of the future Versilov. The little boy commits suicide by drowning, an episode which apparently develops into the suicide of the little boy in Makar's story.[27] In a later version Liza has an affair with a young Prince who shoots himself.[28] In the final version of the novel Prince Sergei Sokolsky contemplates suicide but Liza saves him.[29] In one of the early drafts even the future narrator (the Minor) contemplates suicide.[31]

A Raw Youth is the only novel by the mature Dostoevsky in which there is no single murder. Instead, there are numerous instances of violent self-destruction which are used as structural and compositional devices and as symbols which convey the author's ethical views and religious beliefs.

6. THE BROTHERS KARAMAZOV (BRAT'IA KARAMAZOVY, 1880)

Smerdiakov

There is only one actual suicide in *The Brothers Karamazov*. Pavel Smerdiakov hangs himself after his third fatal interview with Ivan Karamazov. Smerdiakov, the illegitimate son of Fedor Karamazov, is often considered a secondary character in the novel. Yet much of the tragic tension, intrigue and suspense in the novel are generated by his actions.[1] Smerdiakov is a man of few words but his actions, abrupt and extreme, propel the movement of the plot and his suicide, like many of his other deeds and ideas, startle the reader.

Dostoevsky describes Smerdiakov's traits of character at great length, yet the real Smerdiakov eludes us. Dostoevsky compares Smerdiakov with the little peasant in the remarkable picture by Kramskoi, "The Contemplator." Smerdiakov can fall into a trance at any moment and under any circumstance. He keeps his accumulated sensations and impressions hidden from outsiders and even from himself. These perceptions and feelings, which are the product of his psychological make-up and of his life experience, penetrate his subsconscious and guide, at times, his actions and movements.

Smerdiakov, the son of Fedor and the idiot-girl Lizaveta Smerdiashchaia (Stinking Lizaveta) was brought up by the Karamazov's servants Grigorii and Marfa. As a young man of twenty-four he is in the service of Fedor Karamazov who sends him to Moscow to be trained as a cook. Smerdiakov is extraordinarily unsociable, taciturn and secretive. he has a supercilious character and seems to despise everyone. He is a vain man and so vindictive that he can never forget or forgive an insult. He is an epileptic. He exhibits an inborn disposition to sadism. As a boy he was fond of hanging cats and burying them with ceremony. Later in his life he teaches the little Iliusha Snegirov a beastly trick — to take a piece of soft bread, stick a pin into it and then throw it to some stray dog and watch the animals pitiful suffering.

Smerdiakov hates all those who remind him of his origin and rebels against his own birth. He once tells Grigorii that he would have let himself "be killed in the womb rather than come into the world at all."[2] Smerdiakov is always aware of the fact that he is an offspring of the Karamazovs. As an illegitimate child, he belongs to a lower social stratum than that of his brothers whom he treats with hidden disdain. One of Smerdiakov's prime concerns is the task of running away from himself. He has a high opinion of himself, with exaggerated aspirations and expectations from life. He is certain that once people fail to recognize his social stature he will advance in society and assume the place that is his due. He dreams of opening a café-restaurant in Moscow but deep in his heart, he is afraid that word of his true origins will follow him. It appears that old Russia is too small for him, that there is no place where Smerdiakov can escape from his past.

Smerdiakov hates Russia and despairs that the French did not conquer it in 1812: "A clever nation ... would have conquered a stupid one and annexed it. Things would have been different then."[3] Smerdiakov's hope to improve his station in life persists until his final breakdown. During his second interview with Ivan, the latter notices that Smerdiakov studies French words and wonders about the reasons for it. But Smerdiakov clarifies Ivan's doubts without hesitation by saying, "and why shouldn't I learn them, sir? I want to improve my education in case I might one day go to happier parts of Europe myself."[4]

The image of Smerdiakov's mother, Smerdiashchaia Lizaveta, appears first in the drafts of *A Raw Youth*.[5] The character of Smerdiakov is not mentioned in the early stages of Dostoevsky's work on *The Brothers Karamazov*, as long as Ivan is still referred to as "the killer." His name appears for the first time in the drafts when it is inserted next to a notation: "He struck with a knife,"[6] an ominous foreboding which points to Smerdiakov's later role as a parricide. The name, Smerdiakov, is selected for the illegitimate child by Fedor Karamazov himself. This name foreshadows, in a way, the future relationship between father and son. It points to his father's contempt, a fact never forgotten or forgiven by Smerdiakov. The origin and the meaning of the name Smerdiakov, reflect also on the negative ethical and psychological qualities of Smerdiakov's character which are developed fully in the course of his relationship with his father and brothers.

The psychological make-up of Smerdiakov's character is such that he is capable of any action without experiencing pangs of conscience. He is an atheist who fully accepts Ivan's proposition that if there is no God then everything is permitted. He represents, as Ivan says, "excellent material." But even Ivan cannot perceive the extent of Smerdiakov's cunning. It is no wonder that Ivan is unable to properly assess Smerdiakov's intentions and ideas in the beginning. Even during Dmitrii Karamazov's trial, the heated exchange between the prosecutor and the counsel for the defence, indicates clearly their inability to uncover the real character of Smerdiakov. The difference in their perception of Smerdiakov illustrates his complex nature.

To Fetiukovich, Smerdiakov is "a spiteful man, excessively ambitious, vindictive, and violently envious." There is no trace of simplicity in him; his terrible mistrustfulness is "concealed under a cloak of naivety, and an intelligence that was capable of comprehending a great many things."[7] The public prosecutor, on the other hand, characterizes Smerdiakov "as a feeble-minded person with the rudiments of education, confused by philosophic ideas beyond his intelligence."[8] The prosecutor suggests that "people who suffer severely from epilepsy ... are always predisposed to continual and, needless to say, morbid self-condemnation. They worry over their feeling of 'guilt' ... they are tormented by remorse."[9] The public prosecutor rebuffs the allegations of Fetiukovich, ridiculing him for transforming Smerdiakov "into a sort of Byronic hero, who revenges himself upon society for his illegitimate birth."[10] It is obvious that while Fetiukovich is able, at least partially, to unmask the true Smerdiakov, the public prosecutor is totally deluded by Smerdiakov's invincible mask. Even Fetiukovich, however, does not realize the full depth of Smerdiakov's cunning thoughts. During the trial he proceeds with an assumption that Dmitrii did, perhaps, kill his father, but that it was not an intentional murder. The lawyer is carried away by his own eloquence. Basically, he does not believe in Dmitrii's innocence. The whole case is argued in the court on legal, but not moral, grounds. Dostoevsky tries to show that a purely legal approach to justice does not necessarily lead to the truth.

Smerdiakov lives in a state of constant inner rebellion against, what N.M. Chirkov calls, his "source of life."[11] He despises and feels no moral ties with his father, nor does he identify with his brothers. He is an outcast and a coward, doomed to vegetate in Skotoprigonevsk. The spark which turns Smerdiakov's passive inner rebellion into an act of murderous aggression is ignited by his sudden ethical and spiritual identification with his half-brother, Ivan. Until his complete identification with Ivan, Smerdiakov seems apathetic and resigned to his fate. But Ivan's idea that, if there is no God then everything is permitted, corresponds harmoniously with Smerdiakov's own notions about life and God. Moreover, it sets on fire Smerdiakov's smouldering hatred towards his father, turning his inner rebellion into a violent act of murder. Smerdiakov's acceptance of Ivan's atheistic philosophy of life leads to the merger of the latter's ideas with his own bloodthirsty intentions. Smerdiakov is now ready to act because he is confident of Ivan's moral support. His rebellion against his father no longer appears to him as a cowardly act of revenge against his roots, but as an expression of a higher ideal, as an act justified by an elevated notion of life. He now feels he has been given his right to overstep the confines established for him by fate. In murdering his father Smerdiakov believes he will be able to sever his connections with his past life and aspire to new heights along the path indicated by Ivan.

Smerdiakov goes through with the murder of Karamazov. He shrewdly manages to conceal his act. This act will lead to his defeat and final breakdown. He is shortly to realize that his new communion and spiritual unity with Ivan, moulded allegedly by the blood of their dead father, is a delusion. It is a dream which turns into a nightmare. During his last encounter with Smerdiakov, Ivan begins to appreciate the slyness and surprising intelligence of his half-brother, saying "no you're not stupid. You're much cleverer than I thought."[12] At this meeting Smerdiakov discloses to Ivan all the horrifying details of his crime and tells him that he — Ivan — murdered his father: "You are the chief murderer. I was only your accomplice, your loyal page, and I done it because you told me to."[13] Smerdiakov has perceived Ivan's subconscious wish for Fedor Karamazov's death, a wish which the rational Ivan was afraid to admit even to himself. Smerdiakov has acted as an obedient tool of his intellectual mentor, accepting Ivan's departure from town as the tacit approval for the forthcoming murder of Karamazov.

It is this third interview between Ivan and Smerdiakov which leads to Ivan's mental disintegration. Only then does Ivan begin to realize the extent of his guilt as an inspirer of parricide. According to Dostoevsky, evil ideas are even worse than evil deeds. Every individual is "no less responsible for the consequences of the ideas he spreads and propagates than for his own actions."[14] That does not mean in the least that Dostoevsky absolves Smerdiakov of his guilt. Indeed, there are indications that Dostoevsky intends to punish Smerdiakov for his crime. Dmitrii's exclamation, during his meeting with Alesha prior to the trial, that "God will kill him, you will see,"[15] is very ominous in this respect.

Parricide and the miscarriage of justice are at the centre of *The Brothers Karamazov*. These are the problems which receive most attention in literary scholarship. The suicide of Smerdiakov receives surprisingly little notice in the critical literature on the novel. Most critics seem to view Smerdiakov's suicide as an occurrence of little significance to the main plot of the novel. I think that such a conclusion is certainly hasty and ill-founded. The suicide of Smerdiakov has both deep symbolic meaning and important structural impact on the novel; that is, it makes possible the conclusion of the novel along the lines envisaged by the author.

Had Smerdiakov remained alive and been tried for his crime instead of Dmitrii, the symbolic significance attached by Dostoevsky to the conclusion of the Karamazov family drama would have been lost on the reader. Dmitrii's murderous passion, Ivan's murderous ideas and Alesha's passivity, have been transformed into Smerdiakov's murderous act. Dmitrii, Dostoevsky's great tragic hero, accepts collective responsibility for all his brothers. His readiness to accept suffering for the sins of others and his willingness to seek regeneration, if not for actual parricide then for his sinful thoughts and pronouncements, are an expression of Zossima's basic ethical doctrine of man's responsibility for all, and his answer to all other social, hereditary and environmental theories.

Had Smerdiakov not confessed his crime to Ivan, the mystery of parricide would not have been clarified and the evolution of Ivan's character would not have received full expression. Ivan is Dostoevsky's greatest intellectual. His tragedy is expressed in that he cannot accept the limitations of his thought. Smerdiakov's confession leads to Ivan's mental disintegration. After their third interview, the devil — Ivan's hallucination — appears, and Ivan is driven to insanity by the realization of his own guilt. The devil, who is Ivan's double, is the projection of Smerdiakov and a reflection of Ivan. It is even suggested that there is "some evidence that Smerdyakov and the Devil are one."[16]

Ivan is agitated and depressed by Smerdiakov because the latter is the embodiment of what Ivan sees in himself, a projection of Ivan's sense of guilt. Ivan's mental anguish and breakdown are a confession of the bankruptcy of his ideas and the first step to a possible future regeneration. According to Dostoevsky, regeneration is a matter of inner emotion. Only a person who spiritually recognizes something beyond himself is able to regenerate. Ivan, an atheist who is absorbed in constant reasoning and consumed by a sense of unjust suffering of the innocent, could not easily be regenerated. However, there is the possibility that his experiences might lead along the path envisaged by Dostoevsky for Raskolnikov, if not to full regeneration, then at least towards a reassessment of his position in life.

For Dostoevsky, the suicide of Smerdiakov is not only an artistic necessity but also an expression of Dostoevsky's ethics and of his understanding of the nature of man. In the third interview with Ivan we encounter a greatly changed Smerdiakov. "His face had grown very thin and sallow. His eyes were sunken and there were blue patches under them."[17] Smerdiakov returns the stolen money to Ivan and tells him in a shaking voice: "I don't want it at all.... I did have an idea of starting a new life in Moscow or, better still, abroad with that money, but that was just a dream, sir, and mostly because 'everything is permitted.' This you did teach me, sir, for you talked to me a lot about such things: for if there's no everlasting God, there's no such thing as virtue, and there's no need of it at all."[18]

It is evident that Ivan underestimated Smerdiakov's shrewdness. At the same time Smerdiakov overestimated Ivan's strength of character and his ability to witness peacefully his murderous ideas put into action. To discuss abstract ethical and religious principles at the Karamazov dinner table is one thing, but it is a totally different thing to experience the application of these principles in life. Smerdiakov is surprised to learn of "the genuineness of Ivan's horror," which finally strikes him at their last interview, and he mistrustfully questions Ivan, staring at him with a wry smile, "didn't you really know nothing about it?"[19]

Smerdiakov's dream of a better life, which is based on Ivan's ideals and which is to be built on the shattered foundations of the Karamazov family edifice, has been destroyed by Ivan's amazement at, and disapproval of, Smerdiakov's actions. Ivan's rejection does not change Smerdiakov's approach to life. He still refuses to believe in God. He views his murder of Fedor Karamazov as a test of his ability to overstep, as in the case of Raskolnikov, the commonly defined and accepted boundaries of religious and social ethics. By embracing Ivan's abstract notion that if there is no God or immortality then there is no virtue and "everything is permitted," Smerdiakov exemplifies the proposition that ideas once expressed can assume a new life of their own and precipitate actions often unexpected even to those who initiate them.

It appears that Smerdiakov is essentially the creation of Ivan. Wasiolek intimates that Ivan "*makes* Smerdyakov, for Smerdyakov's views are formed largely by the long conversations he has with Ivan."[20] Yet the relationship between the two half-brothers could also be viewed as a conspiracy of master and lackey in which Ivan appears to be the passive partner. In reality, Ivan's ideas provide the murderous impulse and inspiration necessary for committing the crime. Without the moral support of Ivan, Smerdiakov could not have killed his father. His cowardly nature has always been overwhelmed by a sense of insecurity and a fear for his own safety and well-being. As S.I. Gessen suggests "even the external success of the crime cannot overcome the emptiness and dejection of his soul which is dead long since. He had to kill himself without having made peace with the world; without having ever loved anyone in his life; not having even once abandoned his own narrow confines — as a dead mechanism, abandoned by his moving force."[21] Ivan is Smerdiakov's moving force: when Ivan rejects him there is little left for Smerdiakov but death. The changed appearance of Smerdiakov, his state of mind and his total openness with Ivan during their last interview, are all indications of his disillusionment with Ivan and of his disappointment with life — a life which has been inspired by Ivan's ideas. Indeed, soon after Ivan's departure Smerdiakov hangs himself.

Smerdiakov leaves a note which reads: "I put an end to my life of my own free will and no one should be blamed for it."[22] The public prosecutor uses the contents of the note to discredit the allegations of the defence that Smerdiakov is the murderer of the old Karamazov. He says that it would have cost Smerdiakov nothing to add: "I am the murderer, not Karamazov? But he did not add that; did his conscience prompt him to do one thing, but not the other?"[23] There is no clear indication as to whether Dostoevsky initially intended to have Smerdiakov leave a note. At one point, in a statement attributed to the public prosecutor, there is mention in the drafts to *The Brothers Karamazov* of a note similar to that appearing in the final version of the novel. The passage reads: "Now one is pointing to the other. He wrote: I kill myself. Why couldn't he add that he is the murderer?"[24] In another place, however, the counsel for the defence, Fetiukovich decries Smerdiakov's silence. He says: "...'why did not Smerdiakov leave a note: "his conscience prompted him to do one thing, but not the other?" ... Conscience means repentance, but the suicide might not have repented, just despaired. Despair and repentance are two completely different things. Despair might be malicious and irreconcilable'..."[25] Fetiukovich considers Smerdiakov a man incapable of repentance and he says that Smerdiakov is "a wicked creature of intense envy; a man who hates his masters. Why did he not leave a note? He took his vengeance with him into the grave."[26]

It has been pointed out on numerous occasions that the image of Smerdiakov has been created under the influence of West European classics. Thus, for example, V. Komarovich propounds the idea that Javert from V. Hugo's *Les Misérables* serves as a model for the character of Smerdiakov.[27]. Both Smerdiakov and Javert are illegitimate, abandoned children. Both try to run away from their past, both try to avenge themselves on society and finally both commit suicide, although for different reasons.

There are also many parallels between *The Brothers Karamazov* and "The Robbers" by J.Ch.F. Schiller. A.H. Lyngstad points out that Smerdiakov's double crime of murder and suicide "are covered by Franz Moor's analogy between the 'itch' which leads to the conception of a child and the 'itch' to murder; in each case there is nothing but bestiality. If man's life originates in a 'bestial impulse,' who Franz asks, would have any qualms about the 'denial of birth'?"[28] In *The Brothers Karamazov* there are three legitimate brothers and one bastard. In "The Robbers" there are only two brothers. The older, impulsive and dissolute brother, Karl Moor, reminds us of the passionate nature of Dmitrii Karamazov, while the vicious and greedy Franz is more reminiscent of the intellectual Ivan. Yet it is possible to suggest that both Ivan and Smerdiakov inherit certain character traits from Schiller's hero. Ivan, in a way, inherits Franz's ideas, while Smerdiakov follows Franz's examples in action. Smerdiakov is Ivan's murderous tool. Franz Moor puts his ideas into action himself. First he is instrumental in the death of his father, then he strangles himself.[29]

George Steiner suggests that Smerdiakov is in his outward design, "repeatedly associated with Judas."[30] Indeed, there are many parallels between the fates of Smerdiakov and Judas Iscariot which could affirm the treacherous nature of the former. Judas betrays his spiritual father, Christ, to the High Priest Caiaphas and for his deed is awarded thirty pieces of silver. Smerdiakov betrays and murders his blood father, Fedor Karamazov, and robs him of thirty, one hundred ruble notes. When Judas sees that Christ is condemned to die he regrets his act and brings back the silver to the High Priest and the elders, saying that he had betrayed innocent blood. The elders refuse to accept the money and Judas then casts the silver pieces in the Temple and hangs himself.[31] Judas first rejects Christ, his spiritual father, being in turn, himself rejected by the High Priest. Smerdiakov, on the other hand, first rejects his blood father, assuming at the same time the role of both judge and executioner, and is later himself rejected by his spiritual brother, Ivan.

Both Judas and Smerdiakov return the money gained by their treacherous and murderous deeds. Judas returns it to the High Priest, while Smerdiakov returns it to Ivan, his own priest and inspiration. But here ends the parallel between Smerdiakov and Judas, because having rejected Christ and being rejected by the High Priest, Judas hangs himself in despair, exhibiting thus a sign of remorse for his transgression. Smerdiakov also hangs himself, but he does not repent. His suicide should be viewed rather as an act of spiteful vengeance against both his spiritual and blood brothers. His final act of self-destruction should probably be regarded only as a sign of despair rather than of true remorse. Smerdiakov is unable to rise above the level of his own vileness and accept something beyond himself as Judas apparently does. Smerdiakov's suicide, therefore, should be viewed not as a personal tragedy, but rather as a statement of his beliefs and an expression of his character and his free will.

Although there are vague allusions to Smerdiakov's possible repentance in the novel, the evidence to the contrary is more convincing. In the course of his last conversation with Ivan, Smerdiakov asserts that God is among them, yet he denies that he returns the money because he believes in God.[32] The book *Isaac the Syrian* (previously in the possession of Karamazov's servant, Grigorii Kutuzov), which is about a monk and ascetic and one of the earliest theoreticians of Christian mysticism, is on the table next to Smerdiakov's sofa. Smerdiakov places the stolen money under the book before returning it to Ivan. These are obvious hints at Smerdiakov's interest in problems of faith in the last days of his life. As R. Peace points out, there are also numerous allusions to Smerdiakov's identification with the sect of the Castrates and a suggestion "that the murder itself has strong overtones of an act of religious fanaticism."[33] Even though Smerdiakov may be said to be preoccupied with the problems of religion and with God, his preoccupation is not within the confines of conventional Russian religious beliefs. His sectarianism may be said to be an extension of his personal rebellion against, and a refutation of, his roots in the all-important sphere of religion.

It is suggested that "being killed is the extreme form of *submission* just as killing is the extreme form of *aggression*."[34] Smerdiakov's suicide, however, is not an act of submission; it is rather an act of spiteful rebellion against his brothers. For all practical purposes Smerdiakov avenges himself on his blood and kin twice. The first time he avenges himself on his father for bringing him into this world and for placing him in an inferior social position. The second time he avenges himself on his brothers who hate him and treat him with the contempt worthy of a lower human creature. Smerdiakov's rebellion against his father leads to parricide. The rebellion against his brothers leads to suicide, resulting in the conviction of Dmitrii and the mental disintegration of Ivan.

The Freudian analyst Karl Menninger suggests that suicide must be regarded as a peculiar kind of death which entails three internal elements: the wish to kill, the wish to be killed, and the wish to die.[35] Smerdiakov certainly has the wish to kill. He calculates the murder of Karamazov with cold-blooded aloofness. The wish to be killed, which is paradoxically not always tantamount with the wish to die, is expressed in Smerdiakov's defiance of his own being and of his roots. The wish to be killed, which is an assertion of

Smerdiakov's revolt against his own life and of his rebellion against his brothers, leads to his suicide which is the final act of defiance and expression of extreme self-will.

The death of Smerdiakov illustrates the proposition that social decay, expressed in the depraved essence of the Karamazov family and spiritual corruption, exemplified by Smerdiakov's vacuous nature, both lead to biological disintegration symbolized in Smerdiakov's death. The suicide of Smerdiakov demonstrates that the violation of the code of ethics, which separates man from beast and which makes the cohabitation of men on this planet possible, leads to punishment. Smerdiakov is unable to overcome the impelling power of the law of ethics. No one can build his happiness on the misfortunes of others. There are many, according to Dostoevsky, who dare to overstep the boundaries of these unwritten laws but there are very few who are capable of bearing the guilt and responsibility of their crimes and sins. In everyone there are traces of a hidden conscience — a conscience which may sometimes rebel against the rational wishes of its bearer. But Smerdiakov is able to suppress all positive inclinations of his nature. He hangs himself without having publicly repented or atoned for his crime. His suicide is an expression of his evil nature, but his death symbolically signifying the defeat of evil.

Even the knowledgeable reader may be caught off guard by Smerdiakov's suicide, though surprise is a literary device successfully applied by Dostoevsky on numerous occasions. Yet, the suicide of Smerdiakov is so abrupt and unexpected that the question may arise whether it is psychologically convincing and true to life. Despite the fact that suicide is never mentioned as a possible course of action for Smerdiakov, his psychological make up, his physical and mental condition, and his state of mind during his last meeting with Ivan, indicate the possibility of hidden self-destructive inclinations in his personality. Smerdiakov is an epileptic. As such he is predisposed to sleeplessness, melancholia and depression, conditions which usually activate and amplify dormant self-destructive impulses. Various psychoanalytic theories attempting to explain the reasons for suicide throw light on the possible stimuli inducing Smerdiakov to kill himself. It is suggested that "life makes sense in terms of various role constructs; when these have been invalidated, life no longer makes sense."[36] Furthermore, "loss of a symbiotic relationship in which the person has been very dependent on another for self-esteem contributes to suicidal impulses."[37]

According to S. Freud, "perhaps no one can find the psychic energy to kill himself unless in the first place he is thereby killing at the same time someone with whom he had identified himself, and is directing against himself a death wish which had previously been directed against the other person."[38]

In his discussion of Adler's theory of suicide, Heinz L. Ansbacher refers "to the veiled aggression of the suicidal person and his desire to hurt others by injuring himself. Suicide is an act of reproach or of revenge in that it takes the form of veiled attacks on others who will be most affected by it."[39] It is apparent that Smerdiakov's sense of possible fulfillment and his hope for a better future are closely connected with his reliance on Ivan. Once Ivan rejects him, his mental anguish and depression bring to the fore his hidden hatred for his brothers which triggers into action his latent self-destructive instincts.

The suicide of Smerdiakov could also be discussed in the context of the classic murder-suicide situation. In England and Wales one murder in three is followed by a suicide.[40] There are different theories explaining the reasons for the aggressor's self-destruction, but according to one view "the act of suicide, far from being a passive renunciation, constitutes a violent explosion of aggression which is directed against the self only because lack of opportunity or moral restraints prevent the killing of the person responsible for arousing anger.[41]

The suicide of Smerdiakov fits in neatly with most of the above theories. Smerdiakov is, first of all, an epileptic, suffering from psychotic depression. Secondly, he is alienated from his immediate environment; he sees no meaning in his life, no hope for a better future. Thirdly, his suicide is an act of aggression in which he gives vent to his resentment and anger towards his brothers. Finally, it is an act of revenge against Ivan who at first gives rise to his hopes and expectations and later rejects and abandons him to his fate.

Smerdiakov is the only character who kills himself in *The Brothers Karamazov*, but Dostoevsky makes passing reference to suicide in the novel on a number of different occasions. For example, in relating Grushenka's life story to Alesha, Katerina says that after Grushenka was seduced and abandoned by the army officer she "was about to throw herself into the river,"[42] and it was the old merchant Samsonov who actually saved her from death. In another place, the little She-Devil, Liza Khokhlakov, startles Alesha when she exclaims "I'll kill myself because everything is so loathsome to me!"[43] And then, threatening to poison herself,[44] she gives Alesha a secret note for Ivan demanding that it be delivered immediately.

More important by far is the contemplated suicide of Dmitrii Karamazov. On his way to Mokroe in his pursuit of Grushenka who goes there to meet her first love, the widowed officer, Dmitrii is on the brink of suicide. His pistol is loaded. A note in which he says that "I'm punishing myself for my whole life, my whole life I punish!"[45] is in his waistcoat pocket. He makes a rational decision that there is nothing left for him to live for. His conscience is troubled by the innocent blood he shed, for he is sure that he killed his father's servant Grigorii. His pride is hurt and he is extremely ashamed that he could not return the money he had taken from Katerina. In addition, his most passionate life's dream has been destroyed; Grushenka's first love, "the rightful one," has returned; and Dmitrii believes that in losing Grushenka, his whole life will have no meaning.

Unlike Ivan, Dmitrii believes in God. He knows, moreover, that suicide is a great sin. He prays to God, in what are to be the last minutes of his life: "O Lord, receive me with all my lawlessness, and do not judge me.... Do not judge me because I've condemned myself. Do not judge me because I love thee, O Lord. I am vile, but I love thee: if thou sendest me to hell, I shall love thee there, and from there I shall cry that I love thee for ever and ever."[46] Dmitrii does not kill himself on his way to Mokroe. His inherent desire to live is stronger than his rational decision to do away with himself. He still harbours some hope for the future and he wants very much to see Grushenka at least once more, before he takes this final desperate measure.

Dmitrii's arrival in Mokroe changes his perspective on life. Grushenka's encounter and disillusionment with the officer bring hope to his heart. Life has acquired new meaning for him. He prays now not for his own soul but for the health of Grigorii whose life and health are now his great concern and in the way of his happiness. Dmitrii could have made a rational decision to shoot himself. He could have, in a moment of desperation, killed himself impulsively. But Dmitrii survives because he is very much a man of "this" world. He is the very embodiment of man's natural and passionate attachment to life. Dmitrii is dissolute, wicked and low, but he believes in God and he is ready to submit to His judgement. He is prepared to admit his guilt and to repent for his sins and transgressions. He is ready to atone, to accept suffering not only for his own wrongdoings but for the sins of his brothers as well. With all his human shortcomings, Dmitrii is still redeemable. There is, therefore, no need for him to end his life in an act of violent, physical self-destruction.

IV. THE DIARY OF A WRITER (DNEVNIK PISATELIA, 1873-81)

The suicides described in *The Diary of a Writer* can be classified into three distinct categories. Firstly, there are factual accounts of and commentaries on suicides which have taken place in real life. This category includes the suicides of Misha, a young high school student; General Hartung, a member of the upper classes; Pisareva, a young woman of socialist views; the seventeen year old daughter of the well-known Russian émigré, A. Herzen[1]; and Maria Borisova[2], a poor young seamstress. Comprising the second category is a work of fiction based on actual events reported in the daily papers and commented on in *The Diary*. This category is represented by the story "The Meek One" (*Kvotkaia*) inspired by the report of the suicide of the seamstress, Borisova. The last category includes works of fiction which can be classified as philosophical allegories in which physical self-destruction is at the centre of the plot. The significance of such works is mainly symbolic; their chief purpose is to convey a certain idea to the reader. Two stories, "The Verdict" (*Prigovor*) and "The Dream of a Strange Man" (*Son smeshnogo cheloveka*), fall into this category.

Young Misha, a twelve or thirteen year old high school pupil, hangs himself on his saint's day after having been punished by his school-master for failing to learn the lesson. Dostoevsky reflects on the possible reasons for the boy's suicide. Misha has a craving for warmth and love which neither the school nor his parents have satisfied. We are told that the boy is deeply afraid of his father, a very severe man. He hangs himself because he wants to escape shame and further humiliation. What Dostoevsky seems to consider most important, is that Misha's predicament is a reflection of a social malady which is expressed in the lack of communication and understanding between teacher and pupil and between parent and child. To Dostoevsky, the boy's suicide is the result of a way of life "which is in a state of decomposition"[3] leading, in turn, to the disintegration of the family.

The suicide of General Hartung is triggered by an accusation of embezzlement for which he stands trial in Moscow. After the jurors pronounce him guilty and while the court is deciding on the sentence, the General shoots himself. He leaves a note saying that he is not guilty and that he forgives his enemies. In the past, General Hartung had been on friendly terms with a now deceased tailor and money leander. Hartung had readily assumed the role of his executor. It appears that the General entered, perhaps even unknowingly, into collusion with one group of heirs to the detriment of the others. Although Hartung is certainly guilty of breaking the law, he does not consider himself a guilty man. In the eyes of his peers, Hartung is seen as a brave man who is ready to sacrifice his life in order to save his honour — a man who is a victim of circumstances and of his own inexperience rather than a conniving criminal.

The suicide of Hartung provokes Dostoevsky's discussion on the mentality and way of life of Russian upper class society. Dostoevsky does not absolve Hartung of his guilt but, in a way, he excuses him for his transgressions. He claims that as a member of the Russian intelligentsia, Hartung is burdened with the negative traits characteristic of his class. He is ill-equipped to cope with the everyday pressures of modern life. Dostoevsky suggests that Hartung's predicament should not be viewed as a mistake on anyone's part: the General does not consider himself in the wrong nor are the jurors mistaken in their decision. According to Dostoevsky, Hartung's suicide is the result of the workings of blind fate, that is, "a tragedy occurred; blind force, for some reason, chose to punish Hartung alone for the *vices* which are so common in his circle."[4] Dostoevsky goes even further by saying that "one feels sorry for Hartung; but here it is rather a tragedy (very deep tragedy) — the destiny of Russian life, than an error on anyone's part. Or to put it better: here everybody is guilty: the habits and customs of our educated society; the characters which have developed and formed themselves, and finally, the habits and customs of our adopted, young and insufficiently Russified courts. However, if everybody around is guilty this means that individually and singly no one is guilty."[5]

Dostoevsky's explanation of Hartung's suicide is plausible. The General is a product of his society, a child of his age unable to come to terms with the changing world. Consequently he pays with his life for being incapable of adapting to the new realities of his social existence. But Dostoevsky's inference that since all Russians are to be blamed for the poor state of society, no individual should be censured for his personal deeds, is a most un-Dostoevskian conclusion. To absolve the individual from personal responsibility means to deprive him of personal dignity and self-respect. To his credit, General Hartung kills himself not because he lacks self-respect; to the contrary, his exaggerated sense of self-esteem makes him blind to the realities of his immediate environment. The General is guilty of his own downfall. Instead of attempting to become the master of his own destiny, he glides along the path of least resistance becoming a passive tool of blind fate.

The suicide of Pisareva is reported by Dostoevsky in the context of his discussion of the women's question. Women, according to Dostoevsky, are the great hope of Russia. Unfortunately most of them do not believe in any formula of honour and are oppressed by inappropriate ideas. "In Russia an idea crashes upon a man as an enormous stone and half crushes him. And so he shrivels under it, knowing not how to extricate himself. One fellow is willing to live, though in a half-crushed state; but another one is unwilling and kills himself."[6] Pisareva is a woman who is first attracted to, and later crushed by, the ideas of progress. A daughter of a formerly well-to-do landowner, she wants to be useful to society and pays tribute to her socialist views by becoming a midwife. Pisareva is in no need of anything, and she is able to earn a decent living, "but she grew *tired*, very tired — so tired that she decided to take a rest. 'And where can one rest better than in a grave?' "[7]

Indeed, extreme weariness of life and the meaninglessness of existence induce Pisareva to poison herself. The horror of death has become, for her, more alluring than the terror of a tedious life. The reasons for Pisarev'a suicide are obvious to Dostoevsky. "Having lost all faith in truth, all faith in any kind of duty; in a word — a total loss of the sublime ideal of existence,"[8] she puts an end to her life apparently without hesitation. The absence of a "sublime ideal of existence" is for Dostoevsky inseparably linked with lack of faith and with the dearth of a spiritual life based on religious values. "The lack of education, poor upbringing in the family from early childhood, generous inclinations coupled with poorly developed intellect,"[9] are, according to Dostoevsky, other causes which impel misguided people, such as Pisareva, to seek relief from life in physical self-destruction.

The personal tragedies of Herzen's daughter and of the poor seamstress Borisova are discussed in the short piece entitled "Two Suicides" (*Dva samoubiistva*).[10] Here Dostoevsky contrasts two distinct suicides. Two girls of different backgrounds, upbringing and social status, decide to kill themselves for different reasons, yet both suffer and die in apparent anguish. Miss Herzen "soaked a piece of cotton in chloroform, tied it around her face and lay down on the bed.... And thus she died. Before she died, she wrote the following note.... 'I am undertaking a long journey. If I should not succeed, let people gather to celebrate my resurrection with a bottle of Cliquot. *If I should succeed*, I ask that I be interred only after I am altogether dead, since it is very disagreeable to awake in a coffin in the earth. It is not *chic*!' "[11]

The initial account of this suicide is limited to its bare facts. Dostoevsky does not discuss here the external reasons for the girl's decision to kill herself, nor does he imply that her deed is an oblique expression of revolt against her upbringing and against the values prevailing in her parents' home. A more detailed discussion of the above suicide is given in an article appearing several months after the initial publication of "Two Suicides." In the form of a reply to a letter from a certain Mr. N.P., Dostoevsky analyses the state of mind and mood of the girl prior to her final, tragic step. The suicide note expresses a mixture of perversity and despair and the spiteful mood of the girl in the last moments of her life, but it also bears witness, according to Dostoevsky, "to the suffering and painful mood of her spirit."[12] Dostoevsky hypothesizes in his article that the girl dies of anguish "and of aimlessness of life, only because of her upbringing, perverted by theory, at her parents' home — an upbringing involving an erroneous conception of the sublime significance and aims of life, a deliberate extermination in her soul of all faith in its immortality."[13]

It appears that the life of this young girl has been terminated by self-inflicted means, not because she has been in want of anything but rather because she could not transcend the confines of her material world and seek spiritual strength in faith. As on numerous other occasions, Dostoevsky reproaches the parents of the young for failing to instil in their children religious values and a faith in immportality which would make their lives meaningful and bearable.

As opposed to the well-to-do and well-educated daughter of the Russian émigré, the young seamstress described in the "Two Suicides" is so destitute that life becomes simply impossible for her. She is "utterly unable to find work for her livelihood."[14] She kills herself by jumping out of a fourth floor window. Dostoevsky refers here to the suicide of a certain Mar'ia Borisova, previously reported in the Petersburg newspaper *The Voice* (*Golos*). What strikes Dostoevsky most is that she "jumped and fell to the ground, *holding a holy image in her hands*,"[15] as if asking forgiveness from the Lord before the sinful act of suicide has even been committed. "This was a timid and humble suicide. Here, apparently, there was no grumbling or reproach."[16] Her suicide is but a simple admission that the life of suffering has become totally unbearable. The poor seamstress dies in peace. She does not spite anyone. She accepts fate and her faith in immortality gives her the necessary courage and strength to take this last step.

The comparison of the fates of the two unfortunate girls illustrates the proposition that once man satisfies his material needs he must fill his spiritual void in order to be able to sustain a meaningful life. But when man is hungry his first preoccupation is with earthly bread. The "Two Suicides" illustrates clearly that it would be a mistake to ascribe, as Dostoevsky much too often does, self-destructive tendencies primarily to non-believers. Both atheists and fervent believers may have hidden subconscious self-destructive inclinations and thus both have the potential for committing suicide. The two girls kill themselves for different reasons, but one has faith, while the other has none. Regardless of these differences, the balance between the external causes motivating their suicides and the internal instincts driving them to self-destruction is, in both cases, such that they are ready and able to put an end to what seems to be a useless or an extremely difficult existence.

The fate of the poor seamstress does not leave Dostoevsky in peace. It vexes his mind continuously, giving him the necessary impulse for the creation of "The Meek One" (*Krotkaia*).[17] There is no question that the fate of Borisova has inspired the image of the nameless heroine of this new story. Borisova and the "meek one" out an end to their lives in identical fashion. The seamstress jumps out of a window and falls to the ground holding a holy image in her hands; the "meek one" "took a step, pressing the image to her breast — and leaped out of the window."[18] Dostoevsky uses the bare facts from the report of Borisova's suicide and presents the reader with a work of artistic fiction. Here the motif for suicide is combined with the motif of unhappy family life; violent self-destruction serves as a compositional device which unites the beginning and the conclusion of the narrative.

The story is a monologue in the form of a stream of consciousness sequence by a man of over forty who has married a poor girl of sixteen. As the corpse of his dead wife lies in the next room, the man becomes engrossed in recollections about his past and about his relationship with his deceased wife. Immediately after their marriage the girl wants to shower her husband with tenderness and love. He is overwhelmed by her emotional outburst, but he is stern and rejects her advances. He wants to teach her respect and restraint, curtailing her irrational impulses of devotion and love. Once he repels and hurts her sensitive soul, she rebels against his oppressive nature. She turns her back on him, rejecting him forever. They continue living under the same roof but as total strangers.

This psychological confrontation between husband and wife leads to absolute alienation which finally drives the young woman to her death. She cannot accept the love which the lonely and humbled husband tries later to force upon her. She is unable to live a lie and she is too meek and gentle to fight him openly. At one point she contemplates murder. She even puts a gun to his head, but fate spares him and she does not kill him: "The real reason for her faltering hand is her moral nature, her recoil before crime, her refusal, or inability, to transgress."[19] Instead, she chooses her own death, preferring it to further humiliation.

The narrator is apparently biased in his rendition of the story although there is no doubt that he tells about the fate of two unhappy creatures, each of them trying to cope with his difficulties in a different manner, each facing reality on different terms. The narrator cannot fathom the reasons for his wife's suicide, neither can he accept her death in a composed manner. He is terrified by his loneliness and isolation. He would now be prepared to accept the fact that she hates and despises him. He would even be ready to acquiesce in her love for another man, if only she were still alive.

The meek one kills herself because of her psychological alienation. She is utterly alone in a world full of people. She wants to love and be loved, but she cannot love her husband any more. He, on the other hand, has no need of spiritual or social intimacy. All he needs is a physical closeness to someone he can domineer and bully. He appears to be a petty tyrant, a man hurt in his youth who is now trying to oppress his helpless spouse without actually realizing that he drives her to self-destruction by making her life unbearable. He does not realize that his character and conduct are destructive. Thus, the pathetic story about the suicide of the poor seamstress Borisova has been recreated by Dostoevsky into a narrative which manifests not only that man is often unable to understand his fellow man, but that he is even less able to understand himself. This suicide has been reconstructed into a story "about the richness and subtleness of the human soul and about the horror of loneliness and the dramatic effect of alienation."[20]

Both Borisova and the "meek one" kill themselves in a manner which attests to their traditional religious beliefs. We know little about the background of the poor seamstress, but the "meek one" exhibits her adherence to old Russian customs by refusing a modern "English" wedding as her husband requests, insisting rather that the old Russian wedding rituals be observed. Except for the fact that both jump to their deaths holding holy images in their hands, there is little in common between the fates of the two women. The seamstress kills herself because she is destitute; the reasons for her suicide are economic and social. The "meek one" kills herself because of emotional frustration; her suicide arises out of thwarted expectations and an unfulfilled need for personal intimacy. She experiences an inner spiritual emptiness which can be satisfied not by turning to religious faith, but rather by identifying with her fellow man. According to R.L. Jackson, the murder contemplated by the "meek one" shatters her emotional and spiritual equilibrium. She is overcome by a guilty conscience, which together with other causes, provides the final impetus to suicide.[21]

Dostoevsky, the great artist and firm believer in Christ, is truthful to life by revealing in "The Meek One" that suicide is not necessarily a unidimensional phenomenon and that even faith in immortality is not always able to save man from himself. Furthermore, we learn from the fate of the "meek one" that spiritual fulfillment is determined not only by man's religious beliefs but also by man's way of life, his relationship with other people and the ethics of his daily existence. Religious belief and faith in immortality can help man to live a useful life, but it is not always able to prevent him from inflicting death upon himself.

The suicides of the "meek one" and of the poor seamstress, her prototype, stand apart in a way from most other suicides discussed in *The Diary of a Writer* because they question one of Dostoevsky's basic premises — the idea that young people are driven to suicide by their irreligiosity and lack of faith in the immortality of their souls. This premise is vigorously postulated by Dostoevsky in "The Verdict" and "The Dream of a Strange Man" as well as in his dialogue with the reading public, generated by the appearance of the above works.

"The Verdict" is a "confession of a suicide, recorded by himself immediately before he shot himself with a pistol — recorded for his justification and, maybe, as a moral."[22] The narrator rebels against his helplessness in the struggle with the dark forces of nature. He refuses to submit to the elements, and he decides to kill himself in protest. The narrator of "The Verdict" is reminiscent of other early Dostoevskian fictional heroes. He echoes Ippolit when he asks: "Indeed, what right did this nature have to bring me into this world pursuant to some of the eternal laws? I am created with consciousness and I did *conceive* nature: what right had she, therefore, to beget me without my will, without my will as a conscious creature."[23]

The narrator decries the fact that he is unhappy because he is a conscious, thinking creature. He echoes the underground man when he asks: "Look: who is happy in this world and what kind of people *consent* to live? — Precisely those who are akin to animals and come nearest to their species by reason of their limited development and consciousness."[24] The underground man also divides people into two distinct categories: the stupid man of action and the man of higher consciousness. Consciousness for the underground man is a sickness which leads to the realization of man's own helplessness and to total inertia. The underground man is unable to change the world but nor can he accept it as it is. Instead, he escapes reality by spitefully hiding in his physical and mental underground. His escape is tantamount to spiritual self-destruction.

The narrator of "The Verdict" is also a man of higher consciousness. He understands life well but he refuses to accept it. He escapes reality by committing a "logical" suicide. He emulates the underground man by refusing to be a piano key — a blind tool of the dark forces of nature which disregard his personal decisions and trample upon his innermost desires. The awareness of his own helplessness and the futility of his existence drive him to suicide. He contends that:

> "inasmuch as to my question on happiness I am receiving from nature, through my own consciousness, only the answer that I can be happy not otherwise than within the harmony of the whole, which I do not comprehend, and which, it is obvious to me, I shall never be able to understand?... Inasmuch as nature not only does not admit my right to demand an account from her, but even gives me no answer whatsoever — and not because she does not want to answer, but because she is unable to give me an answer.... And because I am unable to destroy nature, I am destroying only myself, weary of enduring a tyranny in which there is no guilty one."[25]

The narrator's idea of the negation of existing reality and of the disharmony between the powerful forces of nature and individual man, is developed with such force that many readers of *The Diary* have failed to notice the author's intended message and have assumed the narrative to be a justification of suicide. In consequence, Dostoevsky has been impelled to clarify his approach to suicide by defining it not only as a sociological, psychological and economic question, but primarily as a religious one. Dostoevsky disassociates his views from those expressed by the narrator of "The Verdict" because he regards the notion of self-destruction as absurd, as an act contrary to human nature and to the ethics of the Russian Orthodox Church.[26] But if one is to apply Albert Camus' definition of the term "absurd"[27] to the interpretation of the actions of the narrator of "The Verdict," one has to conclude that the narrator is not an absurd man, but rather a man who is faced with an absurd problem. According to Camus "it is possible to be Christian and absurd. There are examples of Christians who do not believe in future life."[28]

According to Dostoevsky, the solution to this absurd problem is to be sought in Christian faith and the belief in the immortality of the soul. Dostoevsky emphasizes this thesis most strongly in his indirect reply to Mr. N.P., who has written a politely denunciatory article, published in a Moscow weekly, in which he questions the purpose of printing the deliberations of a half-crazy man.

In the introductory lines to "The Verdict," Dostoevsky notes, as if by the way, that the forthcoming narrative does not contain the deliberations of a half-crazy man or of a man in delirium, but rather "the deliberations of a suicide *out of tedium* — of course, a materialist."[29] According to Dostoevsky, a materialist is most probably an atheist who does not believe in the immortality of the human soul. He is a man whose life is aimless because he realizes that the inert laws of nature will inevitably reduce him to nothingness. According to Dostoevsky, only the hope given by faith in immortality can save man from self-destruction: "without faith in one's soul and its immortality, man's existence is unnatural, unthinkable, impossible."[30] Dostoevsky propounds further the notion that "neither man nor nation can exist without a sublime idea. And on earth there is *but one* sublime idea — namely, the idea of the immortality of man's soul."[31] Therefore, Dostoevsky is convinced that regardless of the external reasons causing man's self-destruction "the majority of the suicides, *in toto*, directly or indirectly, were committed as a result of one and the same spiritual illness — the absence in the soul of these men of the sublime idea of existence."[32]

Dostoevsky's reply to the critics of "The Verdict" took several different forms. At first, he wrote several articles in which he discusses and explains his general approach to the problem of suicide.[33] Several months later, Dostoevsky came forth with what appeared to be an artistic reply to his critics. "The Dream of a Strange Man," published in the April 1877 issue of *The Diary*, was intended to be such a reply. Like "The Verdict," "The Dream of a Strange Man" is written in the confessional style and is narrated by a would-be suicide. The narrator, a young, poor but educated man, is regarded by all as a ridiculous fellow. He himself realizes that he is strange, because his outlook on life appears to be different from that of most others. He is overwhelmed by a terrible anguish brought upon him by a conviction that it is all the same to him whether the world really exists or whether its existence is just a mirage. He is convinced that there has been nothing in the past and that there will be nothing in the future. He decides to shoot himself because he has become completely indifferent to everything. Life is meaningless. Nothing matters any more.

Just like the narrator of "The Verdict" the strange man is a rational man of a higher consciousness, but he is puzzled and disturbed by an irrational and impulsive feeling of guilt for not having helped a poor little girl in need. His rational and logical mind tells him: what difference does it make whether he helped the girl or not since nothing really matters and since he has already made up his mind to shoot himself. In his heart, he pities this little suffering creature and he feels a pain that seems strange and incredible in his situation.

The memory of the little girl saves the narrator from physical self-destruction because after meeting her he postpones the implementation of his decision to kill himself. She also saves him spiritually by touching his deeply hidden emotions, uncovering his inner goodness concealed under a thick web of his rational indifference. The strange man *does* commit suicide, but only in his dream. This ostensible suicide brings him back to *real* life. In his dream, instead of shooting himself in the head, as he had previously intended, he shoots himself through the heart. He wants to be utterly annihilated, to destroy not only his mind but also his heart, the source of his emotions. The dream, however, cures the would-be suicide. He learns in his dream that there is life after the grave and that there is Paradise. He becomes aware of the immortality of man. He says that "I saw Truth and I know that men can be beautiful and happy without losing their faculty of living on earth. I refuse and am unable to believe that evil is a normal condition of men. Yet they all laugh at this belief of mine. But how can I help but have faith: I saw the Truth — my mind did not invent it, and I saw it, saw it, and its *live image* filled my soul forever."[34]

It appears that the narrator, whose mind has been clouded by rational deliberations, has a heart after all, a heart which is still capable of positive human emotions. He sees, in his dream, the Truth which has now become his sublime idea and guiding light. There appears to be no need for suicide any more because there is faith in life and in immortality. But should one accept the confession of the strange man without a trace of scepticism — and at face value? In all probability not! Does he not, in his dream, corrupt the inhabitants of the "beautiful world," the paradise, and return to earth to preach the Truth, but not necessarily to live it? It is suggested that "Dostoevsky criticism will always go wrong when it separates Dostoevsky's ideas from those characters who carry the ideas."[35] Therefore, one should heed the view that "it is not the 'ridiculous man' who tells us his fantastic dream, but the author himself, fifty-six year old Dostoevsky, (who) permitted himself at last to fully disclose his 'most incredible' idea, to remain, though for one instant, in the earthly paradise."[36] In line with the above, it would be worthwhile to note the observation that " 'The Dream of the Ridiculous Man' is *blasphemy*" because it "is *his dream*, and it is as good as his motives, and his motives are self-interested."[37] The flicker of irrational pity which the ridiculous man feels for the small girl "is a threat to his conviction that nothing matters, and the dream is his way of coming to terms with this threat.

And he comes to terms with the threat by killing the truth."[38]

Notwithstanding the above interpretations of the strange man's contemplated suicide, R.L. Jackson suggests that "the ridiculous man's impulse to suicide is rooted in spiritual anguish," because according to Dostoevsky, the desire to kill oneself is "an impulse of 'anguish, unconscious, perhaps, for the sublime significance of life.'"[39] Therefore, Jackson asserts that his "own view is that Dostoevsky is not criticizing the utopian mentality in his story but giving embodiment and expression to his own 'law of striving for the ideal.'"[40]

Under closer scrutiny it becomes obvious that the different interpretations of the strange man's contemplated suicide are not so far apart as it might appear. All the critics agree that Dostoevsky's intended artistic reply to the critics of "The Verdict" is not an artistic reply after all, because the views expressed by the strange man are those of Dostoevsky himself rather than those of the narrator. It is possible also to suggest that on the psychological plane, the ridiculous man does not commit suicide because his irrational will to live and his active instinct of self-preservation are stronger than his rational decisions to kill himself. This compels him to go on living despite his initial indifference to life and his rational decision that his existence is absurd.

The suicides depicted by Dostoevsky in *The Diary of a Writer*, regardless of whether they are discussed on a journalistic level or in the form of artistic fiction, are always generated by actual events of daily life. Real life is the source for the main body of works incorporated in *The Diary* as well as a spring board for Dostoevsky's creative imagination. However, works of fiction incorporated in *The Diary* not only are an artistic recreation of reality but also express, more than any other of his works, the philosophic and aesthetic vision of the author and his approach to social and spiritual phenomena. A work of fiction, once perceived and started, can assume an existence of its own and pursue a course independent of objective reality, often even contrary to the rational intentions of its creator. Hence arises the frequent contradictions between Dostoevsky's ideas expressed in his journalistic writings and those encountered in his works of fiction, including those incorporated in *The Diary*.

CONCLUSION

Happy, self-composed, and well-adjusted people are rare in Dostoevsky's fiction. His heroes are usually tense, divided and complex; unable to master themselves or to come to terms with the outside world. Most of them torture and punish themselves or torment and agonize each other.

Many protagonists, in Dostoevsky's pre-Siberian prose, fail to cope with their social environment. They go down to defeat because they cannot overcome the complexities of their own natures. They succumb to internal, often irrational, self-destructive pressures. In Dostoevsky's post-Siberian fiction slow, passive, ruinous submission to fate is replaced by destructive and self-destructive acts of violence which are, most often, an expression of the freedom of choice and extreme self-will of those concerned.

Physical suicide can never be "completely explained by acute situational factors"[1] only. In essence, the study of suicide is an investigation of self-destructive behaviour in man. This statement underscores the inherent connection between the self-destructive behaviour of Dostoevsky's early heroes and the suicides of his major protagonists in the novels. After his return from Siberia Dostoevsky formulates his theory of the potentiality for evil in human nature. Self-destruction and suicide become identified in his works with evil in man. Thus, Dostoevsky's personal experience in Siberia and his new approach to literature which emphasizes the dramatic qualities of his art, facilitate the transformation of the self-destructive propensities of his early heroes into the violent acts of suicide of the protagonists in his mature prose.

An analysis of Dostoevsky's notebooks and early drafts of his novels indicates clearly the writer's appreciation of the great dramatic potential and artistic possibilities of violent death in literature. In the process of his work on the major novels, Dostoevsky frequently experiments with his material. He has different protagonists kill themselves or each other, in a variety of different combinations and on a number of different occasions, before he finally develops the plot and characters which appear on the pages of the finished novels. It is therefore possible to suggest that while Dostoevsky's interest in the subject of suicide encompasses social, philosophical and religious concerns, the initial impulse for the use of suicide in his novels is prompted in most cases by artistic considerations, specifically, the desire to throw an intensely dramatic light on life at its extreme moments.

Twenty-two successful suicides, as well as a number of attempted and contemplated acts of self-destruction, are depicted in Dostoevsky's works. Fifteen suicides are described in his works of fiction, and seven in *The Diary of a Writer*. Out of these seven, in five instances Dostoevsky reports actual events from real life; on two occasions short works of fiction are incorporated in *The Diary*. Of twenty-two suicides, fourteen are males and eight are females, including five children (three girls and two boys). Most suicides are young people, with Kirillov, Stavrogin, Kraft, and Smerdiakov in their twenties. Hanging was the most prevalent means of suicide in nineteenth century Europe. Drowning was next in line. In the works of Dostoevsky, nine suicides hang themselves (five men, one woman, two girls, and one boy); seven shoot themselves (all men); two poison themselves (both women); two drown themselves (one boy and one girl); and two jump out of a window (both women). (See Appendix 1)

People kill themselves in Dostoevsky's novels for a variety of different reasons. For example, the suicides of Kirillov, Kraft and the narrator of "The Verdict" are "logical." They kill themselves to prove a point or in support of a certain theory developed by each of them. The suicides of Svidrigailov, Stavrogin and Smerdiakov are the result of moral bankruptcy, total indifference and weariness of life, but they are also ethical symbols which intimate that no crime or transgression goes unheeded, that everyone has to face, first, the judgement of his conscience, and later the ultimate judgement of Providence. There are also those who are driven to self-destruction by social and economic reasons which have led them to give up all hope for a better life.

A separate group of suicides is formed by little children. The treament of small children by adults in Dostoevsky is a test of the moral fibre of adult society. The suicides of small boys and girls reflect on those who, instead of protecting children, drive them to desperate acts of self-destruction. Two small girls are driven to suicide by Svidrigailov. Stavrogin causes the death of Matresha, and the merchant Maksim Ivanovich, in *A Raw Youth*, causes the suicide of a little boy. These children are driven to death by the abuse and torture of adults, who are to bear full responsibility for the great sin of suicide, as well as for the crime of murder.

There are several attempted suicides involving leading protagonists which are connected with the main plots of the novels discussed. Most important is the unsuccessful endeavour of Ippolit to shoot himself. Ippolit, a would-be "logical" suicide, decides to take his own life in protest against his helplessness in relation to the blind forces of nature. Nikolai Dement'ev's attempt to hang himself complicates the plot of *Crime and Punishment* and reflects on the personality of Raskolnikov. Most puzzling is Versilov's unexpected attempt to shoot himself which is described on the concluding pages of *A Raw Youth.*

There are two important contemplated suicides in the novels of Dostoevsky, namely, that of Raskolnikov and of Dmitrii Karamazov. Raskolnikov's contemplated suicide expresses his desire to escape shame and punishment for his crime; it is a confession of failure. Dmitrii's intended self-destruction is a sign of contrition, defeat, and disappointment with life. But both Raskolnikov and Dmitrii survive because they are close to the Russian soil and thus, for Dostoevsky, they are still redeemable. Raskolnikov regenerates with the help of Sonia. Dmitrii has faith in God; he is willing to suffer, not only for his own sins, but for the sins of his brothers as well.

In many instances in Dostoevsky, suicide — the ultimate attempt to escape life — alternates with an attempt to escape to a foreign country, most often to America. Total physical annihilation is often equated with spiritual disintegration which is the result of severance from the roots, that is, leaving one's native country for foreign lands. Thus, for example, the possibility of leaving Russia is discussed in connection with the fates of Raskolnikov, Svidrigailov, Stavrogin, Dmitrii Karamazov, and Smerdiakov. But only Kirillov and Shatov actually visit America. It appears that the term "America" is used by Dostoevsky on many occasions as a metaphor for escape, spiritual desolation and even total physical destruction.

Most suicides in the works of Dostoevsky, leave notes which reflect on the reasons and consequences of their self-destruction as well as on their personal character traits and their states of mind immediately prior to killing themselves (see Appendix II). Thus, "logical" suicides such as Kraft, the narrator of "The Verdict" and the would-be suicide Ippolit, leave behind manuscripts in which they explain the reasons for their self-destruction. Kirillov explains the ideas which drive him to suicide to his friends and acquaintances. The contents of the note he writes are forced upon him by the scoundrel, Verkhovensky. Notwithstanding the circumstances under which he writes his suicide note, it ends with an oblique reference to the fact that he kills himself because he made up his mind to put an end to his life long ago.

Major characters, such as Svidrigailov, Stavrogin and Smerdiakov, are mysterious and enigmatic. They are murderers. Their notes are brief and to the effect that no one should be blamed for their deaths. It is paradoxical, even puzzling, that murderers who exhibit no trace of a guilty conscience become concerned with the well-being of those who remain alive to the extent that they take full responsibility for their own deaths in order to remove the suspicion from others.

The suicide note of Olia is written in a tone somewhat reminiscent of the note by Herzen's daughter, whose suicide is described in *The Diary of a Writer*. The "meek one" leaves no note at all, but the manner in which she kills herself contains a message in itself.

Dostoevsky's novels illustrate clearly the prevalence of self-destructive instincts in man's nature; however, they also show that, as in real life, no two suicides are exactly alike. The relationship and balance between the will to live and the will to die, between the instinct of self-preservation and the instinct of self-destruction is, in each individual, influenced in a multitude of different ways by internal and external conflicts and circumstances. Therefore, regardless of external similarities in the reasons for suicide, the self-destructive process which culminates in man's self-inflicted death is different in each and every individual.

Dostoevsky's art is tragic in conception. Moreover, self-destructive tendencies, leading to suicide, are traits which are often characteristic of the genre of tragedy. Yet, in Dostoevsky's novels, most of the major characters who commit suicide are not perceived as tragic heroes, rather, as they are seen as people who embody evil. The reader seldom identifies with their causes and fails to sympathize with them. Dostoevsky's early heroes, on the other hand, also ruin themselves but because they are not wicked, the reader feels compassion for them.

Structurally, the murder of, or by, an important protagonist usually occurs in the beginning or in the end of the novel, serving as a device which facilitates the development of the plot and leads to its logical conclusion. Suicide of an important character on the other hand, occurs almost always on the concluding pages of the narrative. It is used as a device and a means of artistic technique which makes possible the removal of a hero whose role has been played out and who retards the further development of the plot. Suicide is also used by Dostoevsky as a compositional device which helps complicate the plot as in *A Raw Youth* or as a starting point for telling a story, as in "The

Meek One." Whatever the structural or artistic force leading to the suicide, Dostoevsky makes sure that the suicides in his novels are true to life and psychologically convincing.

Suicide for Dostoevsky is not simply an artistic necessity. It usually represents the culmination of a rational argument in which physical self-destruction is used to substantiate a certain ideological notion expounded by his heroes. Thus suicide becomes a symbol of deep philosophical, ethical and religious significance and most importantly, a vehicle for the expression of the writer's *Weltanschauung*. The suicide of a major character in a novel by Dostoevsky can be an act of rebellion, revenge, escape or an expression of extreme self-will, but it is rarely a sign of remorse. Those in whom innate positive qualities abound usually survive — they are, according to Dostoevsky, still redeemable and therefore, able to regenerate.

The use of suicide also gives Dostoevsky the possibility of studying the darker side of man's nature, of exploring the deeper levels of consciousness where the struggle between the inherent instincts of life and death, of self-destruction and self-preservation, takes place. According to a number of leading psychoanalysts, there is a deep-seated suicidal tendency in all of us. However, this "self-destructiveness is tamed, and overcome through our healthy identifications, ego defenses, and our constructive habits of living and loving. When the ordinary defenses, controls, and ways of living break down, the individual may easily be forced into a suicidal crisis."[2] "When a man is suicidal, his perspective freezes. He wants to live, but he can see no way. His logic is confused, but he cannot clear his head. He stumbles into death, still grasping for life."[3] Most of Dostoevsky's heroes are in conflict with themselves and in discord with society; many are sick in soul and in body. Their suicidal tendencies, which in ordinary healthy people are hidden deep under the surface, easily come to the fore.

In conclusion, the function of suicide in Dostoevsky's art can be summarized as:

a) a literary device serving to remove a character from the scene;
b) a method to attach ideological meaning to the actions of a character;
c) a symbol of deep philosophical, ethical, or religious significance;
d) a vehicle for the expression of the author's views; and,
e) a means for the exploration of the deeper levels of man's subconscious and the darker sides of human nature.

The application of the above artistic and ideational functions illustrates clearly the meaning and significance of suicide for Dostoevsky, the man and the artist. On the psychological plane suicide in Dostoevsky's art is the highest expression of the irrational self-destructive tendencies prevalent in man's nature. On the philosophical plane, suicide is an expression of evil in human nature which is activated by man's assertion of his freedom of choice which takes the form of extreme self-will and which signifies man's lack of faith and his rebellion against God. Most major characters in Dostoevsky's fiction, who commit, attempt or contemplate suicide, such as for example, Raskolnikov, Ippolit, Kirillov, Stavrogin or Smerdiakov, are unbelievers and they kill or want to kill themselves, in defiance of the commandment "Thou shalt not kill."

In his journalistic writings, Dostoevsky asserts, time and again, that suicidal tendencies are characteristic mostly of socialists and materialists, people who do not believe in the immortality of the soul, and that only faith can move man out of his suicidal preoccupation. And yet, in some of his works, Dostoevsky shows that even religious people are not immune to their own self-destructive instincts and that they are often driven to suicide by different internal and external causes. Thus, as in many other instances, Dostoevsky, the great artist, is true to himself. In his journalistic writings he devises a single, all-embracing formula which is supposed to save man from himself, while in his fiction, he illustrates clearly that man is too complex a creature by far to submit to universal panaceas or to be saved by uni-dimensional solutions to all his problems.

Suicide in Dostoevsky creates intrigue and suspense; it generates interest and helps keep the reader's attention on the narrative to its last page. But it is also a powerful tool which helps the writer penetrate man's psyche and study the dark sides of his soul. It is an effective means to illustrate convincingly the whole complexity of human nature and to attest to the unpredictability of man's fate.

APPENDIX I

APPENDIX I. SUICIDES IN THE WORKS OF DOSTOEVSKY

TITLE	NO.	ACTUAL SUICIDES	ATTEMPTED SUICIDES	CONTEMPLATED SUICIDES	SEX	AGE	MODE
"Diadiushkin son"	1.		Vasia		M.	20s	poisoning
Crime and Punishment	2.	Svidrigailov			M.	50	shooting
	3.	Philip			M.		hanging
	4.	Resslikh			F.	14-15	hanging
	5.	Girl in dream of Svidrigailov			F.	14	drowning
	6.		Demente'ev		M.	young	hanging
	7.		Afrosiniushka		F.	young	drowning
	8.			Raskolnikov	M.	23	drown-shoot
The Idiot	9.	Kapiton Alekseevich			M.	70	shooting
	10.		Ippolit		M.	17-18	shooting
"The Eternal Husband"	11.	Clerk - nameless			M.	young	hanging
The Possessed	12.	Kirillov			M.	27	shooting
	13.	Stavrogin			M.	29	hanging
	14.	Boy - nameless			M.	19	shooting
	15.	Matresha			F.	11	hanging
	16.		Liamshin		M.	young	shooting
A Raw Youth	17.	Kraft			M.	26	shooting
	18.	Olia			F.	young	hanging
	19.	Soldier			M.	retired	hanging
	20.	Boy			M.	young	drowning
	21.		Versilov		M.	47	shooting
The Brothers Karamazov	22.	Smerdiakov			M.	24	hanging
	23.			Dmitrii	M.	29	shooting
The Diary of a Writer	24.	Misha			M.	12-13	hanging
	25.	Pisareva			F.	25	poisoning
	26.	Borisova			F.	young	jumped
	27.	Herzen's daughter			F.	17	chloroform
	28.	General Hartung			M.		shooting
	29.	The meek one			F.	16	jumped
	30.	Narrator in "The Verdict"			M.	young	shooting
	31.			Narrator "The Dream of a Strange Man"	M.	young	shooting

APPENDIX II

SUICIDE NOTES

Most suicides leave a written message to those who survive them. The readers of such notes search there for explicit or implicit explanations of the reasons for self-destruction. Most often, however, a suicide note is written shortly before its author takes his life when, it is presumed, the writer is in a state of emotional excitement and is functioning under heightened motivation. In consequence, encoding the language and the proper interpretation of a note, are of prime importance to gain an understanding of the reasons for the suicide's actions and an appreciation of his state of mind in the last moments of his life.

Theoretical analysis of the effect of motivation level upon encoding leads to several hypotheses. It is suggested that messages produced in suicide notes under heightened drive level should "a) be more stereotyped, b) be more disorganized, if the motivation level is extremely high, c) reflect the specific nature of the motives operating, and d) reflect conflict of response if two or more competing motives are operating."[1]

Crime and Punishment
SVIDRIGAILOV

"He felt in his pocket for the revolver, took it out and correctly replaced the percussion cap; then he sat down, took out a notebook and wrote a few lines in large letters on the front page, where they must be seen, read them over, and sat pondering with his elbows on the table.... He left a few words in a notebook to say that he died in his right mind and to ask that nobody should be blamed for his death."[2]

The Idiot
IPPOLIT

The reasons for Ippolit's intended suicide are given in the manuscript entitled, "My Necessary Explanation."[3]

The Possessed
KIRILLOV

Petr Verkhovensky dictates to Kirillov the following: "I Kirillov declare that to-day, the -th October, at about eight o'clock in the evening, I killed the student Shatov in the park for turning traitor and giving information of the manifestoes and of Fedka, who has been lodging with us for ten days in Filipov's house. I am shooting myself to-day with my revolver, not because I repent and am afraid of you, but because when I was abroad I made up my mind to put an end to my life.... Vive la république démocratique sociale et universelle ou la mort! Liberté, égalité, fraternité ou la mort. De Kirilloff.... Gentilhomme, séminariste russe et citoyen du monde civilisé!"[4]

STAVROGIN

"On the table lay a piece of paper with the words in pencil: 'No one is to blame, I did it myself.' "[5]

NAMELESS YOUNG MAN, NOT MORE THAN NINETEEN

"On the table lay a note, in his handwriting, to the effect that no one was to blame for his death, that he had killed himself because he had 'squandered' four hundred roubles. The word 'squandered' was used in the letter; in the four lines of his letter there were three mistakes in spelling."[6]

A Raw Youth

KRAFT

"He left behind him a manuscript book full of abstruse theories, proving by phrenology, by craniology, and even by mathematics, that the Russians are a second-rate race, and that therefore, since he was a Russian, life was not worth living for him."[7]

OLIA

"Mother darling, forgive me for cutting short my début into life. Your Olya who is causing you such grief."[8]

The Brothers Karamazov

SMERDIAKOV

"On the table was a note: 'I put an end to my life of my own free will and no one should be blamed for it.' "[9]

DMITRII KARAMAZOV

Before his intended suicide he prepared the following note: "I'm punishing myself for my whole life, my whole life I punish!"[10]

The Diary of a Writer

PISAREVA

"Don't lose your head! Don't start crying 'ah!' and 'oh!' Make an effort and read to the end, and then decide what's the best course. Don't frighten Petrova. Maybe nothing will come of it, anyway, except laughter. My passport is in the cover of the trunk.... Do but leave me alone! I am tired! ... Don't forget to pull off me the new shirt and stockings: on my table you will find an old shirt and a pair of old stockings. These should be put on me... Did you really believe that I was going home? What the devil would I go there for? ... Now Lipareva, forgive me, and let Petrova forgive me (it was in the latter's apartment that Pisareva took poison) — particularly Petrova. I am committing a swinish act, a filthy thing.... Don't let Lizanka know, because she will inform sister, and she will come here and will start howling. I don't wish that people should be howling over me, but all relatives without exception howl over their relatives.... Let's hurry, let's get it over as quickly as possible — and let me rest.... Such and such monies should not be taken by the relatives; this sum should be given to Petrova; twenty-five rubles which the Chechotkins loaned me for the journey should be returned to them."[11]

HERZEN'S DAUGHTER

"I am undertaking a long journey. If I should not succeed, let people gather to celebrate my resurrection with a bottle of Cliquot. *If I should succeed*, I ask that I be interred only after I am altogether dead, since it is very disagreeable to awake in a coffin in the earth. It is not *chic*!"[12]

"THE MEEK ONE"

"She didn't even leave a note to the effect: 'Don't blame anyone for my death.' "[13]

GENERAL HARTUNG

"On his person a note — also written beforehand — was found, in which he 'swears by Almighty God that in this case he embezzled nothing, and that he forgives his enemies.' "[14]

"THE VERDICT"

The manuscript is, in a sense, a suicide note explaining the reasons for the narrator's suicide.

"THE DREAM OF A STRANGE MAN"

The manuscript explains the reasons for the narrator's intended suicide.

NOTES

I. INTRODUCTION: SUICIDE IN LIFE AND FICTION

1 The case of Ippolit is an important exception to this rule. For a general discussion of the problem of death in literature see Robert F. Weir, ed., *Death in Literature* (New York, 1980).

2 V.I. Kaigorodov, "Smert' geroev v proizvedeniiakh F.M. Dostoevskogo," *Leningradskii gosudarstvennyi pedagogicheskii institut imeni A.T. Gertsena. XXX gertsenovskie chteniia. Literaturovedenie. Nauchnye doklady* (Leningrad, 1977), p. 36.

3 Leonid Grossman, "Composition in Dostoevsky's Novels," in *Balzac and Dostoevsky* (Ann Arbor, 1973), pp. 62-63.

4 Alfred Alvarez, *The Savage God. A Study of Suicide* (London, 1972), p. 184.

5 A. Steinberg, *Dostoievsky* (London, 1966), p. 28.

6 *Letters of Fyodor Michailovitch Dostoevsky to his Family and Friends.* Translated by Ethel Colburn Mayne (London, 1961), p. 23.

7 F.M. Dostoevsky, *Pis'ma, 1832-1867*, vol. 1, edited and with commentaries by A.S. Dolinin (Moscow-Leningrad, 1928), p. 170.

8 *Ibid., 1878-1881*, vol. 4 (Moscow, 1959), p. 339. One may wonder why Dostoevsky writes in his note "I will soon by fifty." He was born October 30, 1821, and was in January 1873 well over fifty-one. O. Kozlova was the wife of the poet and translator of Byron, Pavel Alekseevich Kozlov (1841-1891). See *Ibid.*, p. 472.

9 Alvarez, p. 132.

10 John Churton Collins, *Studies in Shakespeare* (London, 1904), pp. 162 ff, quoted in James Holly Hanford, "Suicide in the plays of Shakespeare," *Publications of the Modern Language Association of America*, XXVII (1912), p. 380.

11 *Ibid.*, p. 395.

12 *Ibid.*, pp. 395-96.

13 Alvarez, p. 132.

14 Jacques Choron, *Suicide* (New York, 1972), p. 31.

15 Robert J. Havinghurst, "Suicide and Education," in *On the Nature of Suicide*, edited by Edwin S. Shneidman (San Francisco, 1969), p. 57.

16 Choron, p. 31.

17 *Ibid.*

18 Leo Tolstoy, *A Confession. The Gospel in Brief, and What I Believe*, translated by Aylmer Maude (London, 1961), p. 18.

19 Franz Kafka, *The Trial*, translated by Douglas Scott and Chris Waller (London, 1977), p. 254.

20 *Ibid.*

21 Hermann Hesse, *Steppenwolf* (New York, 1974), p. 25.

22 *Ibid.*, p. 100.

23 Albert Camus, *The Stranger*, translated from the French by Stuart Gilbert (New York, 1946), pp. 142-43.

24 *Entsiklopedicheskii slovar'*, izd. F.A. Brokgauz i I.A. Efron, vol. XXVIIIA (S.-Peterburg, 1900), p. 238.

25 A. Dolinin, *V tvorcheskoi laboratorii Dostoevskogo* (1947), pp. 98-99, quoted in D.V. Grishin, *Dostoevsky - chelovek, pisatel' i mify* (Melbourne, 1971), p. 132.

26 *Entsiklopedicheskii slovar'*, p. 238.

27 *Ibid.*, p. 235.

28 Maurice Halbwachs, *The Cause of Suicide*, translated from the French by Harold Goldblatt (London, 1978), p. 59.

29 *Entsiklopedicheskii slovar'*, p. 236.

30 Emile Durkheim, *Suicide. A study in Sociology*, translated by John A. Spaulding and G. Simpson (New York, 1965), p. 58.

31 Arthur Schopenhauer, *The World as Will and Representation*, translated from the German by E.F.J. Payne, vol. 2 (New York, 1966), p. 351.
32 Choron, p. 72.
33 S. Freud, *Standard Edition of the Complete Psychological Works*, vol. 11 (London, 1957), p. 232.
34 S. Freud, *Ibid.*, vol 23 (London, 1964), pp. 148-49.
35 Robert E. Litman, "Sigmund Freud and Suicide," in E.S. Shneidman, and others, compilers, *The Psychology of Suicide* (New York, 1970), pp. 580-81.
36 Karl A. Menninger, *Man Against Himself* (New York, 1938), p. 25.
37 Joseph J. Kockelmans, "On Suicide: Reflections upon Camus' View of the Problem," *Psychoanalytic Review*, vol. 54 (3) (1967), p. 36 (428).
38 Albert Camus, *The Myth of Sisyphus*, translated from the French by Justin O'Brien (London, 1955), p. 11.
39 *Ibid.*, p. 13.
40 *Ibid.*
41 *Ibid.*, p. 57.
42 Albert Camus, *The Rebel* (New York, 1954), p. 6.
43 Leo Tolstoy, *Anna Karenin* (Harmondsworth, 1962), p. 529.
44 H.J. Rose, "Suicide. Introductory," in James Hastings, editor, *Encyclopaedia of Religion and Ethics*, vol. 12 (New York, n.d.), p. 22.
45 *Ibid.*, p. 24.
46 *Ibid.*, p. 23.
47 *Entsiklopedicheskii slovar'*, p. 234.
48 H.J. Rose, p. 22.
49 D.I. Sapozhnikov, *Samosozhzhenie v russkom raskole* (Moscow, 1891), Appendix II.
50 Thomas G. Masaryk, *Suicide and the Meaning of Civilization*, translated by William G. Weist and Robert G. Batson (Chicago, 1970), p. 119.
51 *Ibid.*, p. 141.
52 *Ibid.*, p. 140.
53 Konstantin Mochulsky, *Dostoevsky. His Life and Work*, translated by Michael A. Minihan (Princeton, N.J., 1971), pp. 364-65.

II. SELF-DESTRUCTIVE ELEMENTS IN DOSTOEVSKY'S EARLY WORKS
1. Pre-Siberian Period

1 Victor Terras, "Problems of Human Existence in the Works of the Young Dostoevsky," *Slavic Review*, XXIII (March, 1964), p. 89.
2 Joseph Frank, *Dostoevsky. The Seeds of Revolt, 1821-1849* (Princeton, 1979), p. 148.
3 Fyodor Dostoyevsky, *Poor Folk. The Gambler*, translated by C.J. Hogarth (New York, 1968), p. 75.
4 F.M. Dostoevsky, *Polnoe sobranie sochinenii v tridtsati tomakh*, vol. 1 (Leningrad, 1972), p. 267.
5 *Ibid.*, p. 317.
6 Joseph Frank, p. 338.
7 *Ibid.*, p. 341.
8 F.M. Dostoevsky, *Polnoe sobranie*, vol. 2 (Leningrad, 1972), p. 6.
9 *Ibid.*, p. 40.
10 *Ibid.*,p. 38.
11 *Ibid.*, p. 141.
12 *Ibid.*, p. 157.
13 *Ibid.*, p. 188.
14 Iu. G. Kudriavtsev claims that Netochka's mother commits suicide, evidently

basing his conclusion on the fact that she drinks a glass of wine before going to sleep for the last time, and assuming thus that she poisons herself. See Iu. G. Kudriavtsev, *Tri kruga Dostoevskogo* (Moscow, 1979), p. 21, see also F.M. Dostoevsky, *Polnoe sobranie*, vol. 2, p. 183.

15 Victor Terras, p. 89.

2. Post-Siberian Period

1 E.H. Carr, *Dostoevsky. 1821-1881* (London, 1962), p. 55.

2 F.M. Dostoevsky, *Polnoe sobranie sochinenii v tridtsati tomakh*, vol. 2 (Leningrad, 1972), p. 392.

3 *Ibid.*

4 M.S. Al'tman, "Iz arsenala imen i prototipov literaturnykh geroev Dostoevskogo," *Dostoevsky i ego vremia*, edited by V.G. Bazanov and G.M. Fridlender (Leningrad, 1971), pp. 202-203.

5 Fyodor Dostoyevsky, *The House of the Dead*, translated by Constance Garnett (New York, 1959), pp. 84-85.

6 Konstantin Mochulsky, *Dosteovsky. His Life and Work*, translated by Michael A. Minihan (Princeton, N.J., 1971), p. 172.

7 N.M. Chirkov, *O stile Dostoevskogo* (Moscow, 1963), p. 49.

8 Fyodor Dostoyevsky, *The House of the Dead*, pp. 130-31.

9 *Ibid.*, pp. 75-76.

10 *Ibid.*, pp. 56-57.

11 Robert Louis Jackson, *The Art of Dostoevsky. Deliriums and Nocturnes* (Princeton, N.J., 1981), p. 159.

12 *Ibid.*, p. 9.

III. MAJOR WORKS OF FICTION

1 Fyodor Dostoevsky, *Notes from Underground. White Nights. The Dream of a Ridiculous Man, & Selections from the House of the Dead*, translated by Andrew R. MacAndrew (New York, 1961), p. 92.

2 F.M. Dostoevsky, *Pis'ma. 1832-1867*, vol. 1, edited and with commentaries by A.S. Dolinin (Moscow-Leningrad, 1928), p. 353.

3 F.M. Dostoevsky, *Polnoe sobranie sochinenii v tridtsati tomakh*, vol. 5 (Leningrad, 1973), p. 79.

4 Norman L. Farberow and Edwin S. Shneidman, eds. *The Cry for Help* (New York, 1965), p. 296.

5 Feodor Dostoievsky, *The Diary of a Writer*, translated and annotated by Boris Brasol, vol. 1 (New York, 1949), pp. 538-42.

6 Fyodor Dostoyevsky, *Poor Folk. The Gambler*, translated by C.J. Hogarth (New York, 1968), p. 297.

7 Edwin S. Shneidman, and others, compilers, *The Psychology of Suicide* (New York, 1970), p. 36.

8 *Ibid.*, p. 37.

1. Crime and Punishment

1 Fyodor Dostoevsky, *The Notebooks for "Crime and Punishment,"* edited and translated by Edward Wasiolek (Chicago, 1967), pp. 63-64, and 243-44.

2 Feodor Dostoevsky, *Crime and Punishment*, translated by Jessie Coulson. Edited by

George Gibian (New York: A Norton Critical Edition, 1964), p. 152.

3 *Ibid.*, p. 164.

4 Karl A. Menninger, *Man Against Himself* (New York, 1938), p. 52.

5 A.L. Bem, *Dostoevsky. Psikhoanaliticheskie etiudy* (Praga, 1938), p. 168.

6 *Crime and Punishment*, p. 182.

7 Janko Lavrin, *Dostoevsky* (New York, 1947), p. 97.

8 J. Middleton Murry, *Fyodor Dostoevsky. A Critical Study* (New York, 1966), p. 109.

9 Nicholas Berdyaev, *Dostoevsky*, translated by Donald Attwater (New York, 1962), p. 98.

10 N. Strakhov, "The Nihilists and Raskolnikov's New Idea," in *Crime and Punishment*, edited by G. Gibian, p. 546.

11 *Crime and Punishment*, p. 309.

12 *Ibid.*, p. 521.

13 *Ibid.*, p. 443. According to some critics Porfiry asks Raskolnikov to leave a note in order to arouse in him a feeling of belonging to the human race.

14 *Ibid.*, p. 497.

15 *Ibid.*, p. 501.

16 F.M. Dostoevsky, *Polnoe sobranie sochinenii v tridtsati tomakh*, vol. 7 (Leningrad, 1973), p. 204.

17 Konstantin Mochulsky, *Dostoevsky. His Life and Work*, translated by Michael A. Minihan (Princeton, N.J., 1971), p. 312.

18 V. Ia. Kirpotin, *Razocharovanie i krushenie Radiona Raskol'nikova* (Moscow, 1970), p. 347.

19 N. Strakhov, p. 546.

20 *Crime and Punishment*, p. 277.

21 *Ibid.*, p. 491.

22 *Ibid.*, p. 485.

23 *Ibid.*, p. 286.

24 *Ibid.*, p. 476.

25 *Ibid.*, p. 269.

26 *Ibid.*, p. 273.

27 *Ibid.*, p. 270.

28 V. Ia. Kirpotin, *Razocharovanie*, p. 246.

29 Iu. G. Kudriavtsev, *Tri kruga Dostoevskogo* (Moscow, 1979), p. 35.

30 *Ibid.*

31 *Ibid.*, pp. 211-12.

32 Vladimir Chizh, *Dostoevsky kak psikhopatolog* (Moscow, 1885), p. 76.

33 Richard Peace, *Dostoyevsky. An Examination of the Major Novels* (Cambridge, 1971), p. 51.

34 Philip Rahv, "Dostoevsky in *Crime and Punishment*," in René Wellek, ed., *Dostoevsky. A Collection of Critical Essays* (Englewood Cliffs, N.J., 1962), p. 26.

35 *Crime and Punishment*, p. 277.

36 *Ibid.*

37 *Ibid.*, p. 451.

38 *Ibid.*, p. 452.

39 D.A. Traversi, "Dostoevsky," in René Wellek, ed., p. 166.

40 Natalie Babel Brown, *Hugo and Dostoevsky* (Ann Arbor, 1978), p. 65.

41 *Crime and Punishment*, p. 477.

42 George Gibian, "Traditional Symbolism in *Crime and Punishment*," in Feodor Dostoevsky, *Crime and Punishment*, p. 578.

43 *Crime and Punishment*, p. 491.

44 E.H. Carr, *Dostoevsky. 1821-1881* (London, 1962), p. 152.

45 *Ibid.*, p. 154.

46 *Ibid.*
47 Viktor Shklovsky, *Povesti o proze*, vol. 2 (Moscow, 1966), p. 231.
48 *Ibid.*, p. 265.
49 V. Ia. Kirpotin, *Razocharovanie*, p. 245.
50 Fyodor Dostoevsky, *The Notebooks for "Crime and Punishment,"* p. 82.
51 *Crime and Punishment*, pp. 131-32.
52 L. Grossman, *Dostoevsky*, 2nd ed., corrected and appended (Moscow, 1965), p. 354.
53 M.S. Al'tman, "Iz arsenala imen i prototipov literaturnykh geroev Dostoevskogo," *Dostoevsky i ego vremia*, edited by V.G. Bazanov and G.M. Fridlender (Leningrad, 1971), p. 202.
54 *Crime and Punishment*, p. 436.
55 A.L. Bem, *Dostoevsky*, p. 148.

2. The Idiot

1 F.M. Dostoevsky, *Polnoe sobranie sochinenii v tridtsati tomakh*, vol. 9 (Leningrad, 1974), p. 368.
2 Fyodor Dostoevsky, *The Notebooks for "The Idiot,"* edited by Edward Wasiolek; translated by Katharine Strelsky (Chicago, 1973), p. 236.
3 N.M. Chirkov, *O stile Dostoevskogo* (Moscow, 1967), p. 133.
4 Fyodor Dostoyevsky, *The Idiot*, translated by David Magarshack (Harmondsworth, 1961), pp. 443-44.
5 *Ibid.*, p. 447.
6 *Ibid.*
7 *Ibid.*, p. 450.
8 Konstantin Mochulsky, *Dostoevsky. His Life and Work*, translated by Michael A. Minihan (Princeton, N.J., 1971), p. 362.
9 E.H. Carr, *Dostoevsky. 1821-1881* (London, 1962), p. 168.
10 Edward Wasiolek, *Dostoevsky. The Major Fiction* (Cambridge, Mass. 1971), pp. 96-97.
11 *Ibid.*, p. 98.
12 Fyodor Dostoevsky, *The Notebooks for "The Idiot,"* pp. 234 and 236-39.
13 Fyodor Dostoyevsky, *The Idiot*, p. 430.
14 Fyodor Dostoevsky, *The Notebooks*, p. 239.
15 Fyodor Dostoyevsky, *The Idiot*, p. 460.
16 Alfred Alvarez, *The Savage God. A Study of Suicide* (London, 1972), p. 76.
17 Erwin Stengel, *Suicide and Attempted Suicide* (New York, 1974), p. 87.
18 Fyodor Dostoevsky, *The Notebooks*, p. 18.
19 *Ibid.*, p. 164.
20 Edward Wasiolek, *Dostoevsky*, pp. 88 and 90.
21 Fyodor Dostoyevsky, *The Idiot*, p. 646.
22 F.M. Dostoevsky, *Polnoe, sobranie*, p. 227.
23 *Ibid.*, p. 234.
24 Fyodor Dostoyevsky, *The Idiot*, p. 627.
25 *Ibid.*, pp. 387 and 394.
26 F.M. Dostoevsky, *Polnoe sobranie*, pp. 271-72.
27 *Ibid.*, p. 388.
28 *Ibid.*, pp. 270-73.
29 *Ibid.*, pp. 271 and 274.

3. "The Eternal Husband"

1 F.M. Dostoevsky, *Polnoe sobranie sochinenii v tridtsati tomakh*, vol. 9 (Leningrad, 1974), pp. 50-51.

2 *Ibid.*, p. 41.
3 *Ibid.*, p. 104.
4 *Ibid.*, p. 292.
5 *Ibid.*, p. 299.
6 *Ibid.*, p. 302.
7 *Ibid.*, p. 316.
8 *Ibid.*, p. 478.
9 Alex de Jonge, *Dostoevsky and the Age of Intensity* (London, 1975), pp. 174-75.
10 A.L. Bem, *Dostoevsky. Psikhoanaliticheskie etiudy* (Praga, 1938), p. 71.
11 *Ibid.*, p. 72.
12 *Ibid.*, p. 164.

4. The Possessed

1 Fyodor Dostoyevsky, *The Possessed*, translated by Constance Garnett (New York, 1961), p. 112.
2 *Ibid.*, p. 113.
3 *Ibid.*, p. 132.
4 *Ibid.*, pp. 133-34.
5 *Ibid.*, p. 632.
6 *Ibid.*, pp. 632-33.
7 *Ibid.*, pp. 633-34.
8 F.M. Dostoevsky, *Polnoe sobranie sochinenii v tridtsati tomakh*, vol. 11 (Leningrad, 1974), p. 241.
9 V.I. Kel'siev, *Perezhitoe i peredumannoe* (S. Petersburg, 1868), pp. 386-462, quoted in F.M. Dostoevsky, *Polnoe sobranie*, vol. 12 (Leningrad, 1975), p. 231.
10 L. Grossman, *Dostoevsky*, 2nd ed., corrected and appended (Moscow, 1965), p. 107.
11 F.M. Dostoevsky, *Pis'ma. 1967-1871*, vol. 2, edited and with commentaries by A.S. Dolinin (Moscow-Leningrad, 1930), pp. 474-75.
12 F.M. Dostoevsky, *Polnoe sobranie*, vol. 12, p. 222.
13 B.S. Itenberg, "Revoliutsionnye narodniki i voprosy religii," in *Voprosy istorii religii i ateizma. Sbornik statei*, XI (Moscow, 1963), p. 303, quoted in F.M. Dostoevsky, *Polnoe sobranie*, vol. 12, p. 223.
14 *Ibid.*
15 *Ibid.*, vol. 11, p. 303.
16 F.M. Dostoevsky, *Polnoe sobranie*, vol. 12, p. 222.
17 V.L. Komarovich, " 'Mirovaia garmoniia' Dostoevskogo," in D. Fanger, ed., *O Dostoevskom, Stat'i* (Providence, Rhode Island, 1966), p. 142.
18 F.M. Dostoevsky, *Polnoe sobranie*, vol. 12, p. 222.
19 V.V. Vinogradov, "Iz biografii odnogo 'neistovogo proizvedeniia' (Poslednii den' prigovorennogo k smerti)," in *Evoliutsiia russkogo naturalizma* (Leningrad, 1929), pp. 140-42.
20 Fyodor Dostoyevsky, *The Possessed*, p. 640.
21 V.V. Vinogradov, p. 146.
22 Fyodor Dostoyevsky, *The Possessed*, p. 633. See Appendix for Kirillov's suicide note.
23 Edward Wasiolek, *Dostoevsky. The Major Fiction* (Cambridge, Mass., 1971), p. 123.
24 Fyodor Dostoyevsky, *The Possessed*, p. 134.
25 *Ibid.*, p. 633.
26 *Ibid.*, p. 634.
27 Konstantin Mochulsky, *Dostoevsky. His Life and Work*, translated by Michael A. Minihan (Princeton, N.J., 1971), p. 450.
28 André Gide, *Dostoevsky* (London, 1967), p. 162.

29 *Ibid.*, p. 166.
30 Irving Howe, "Dostoevsky: The Politics of Salvation," in René Wellek, ed., *Dostoevsky. A Collection of Critical Essays* (Englewood Cliffs, N.J., 1962), p. 64.
31 V.F. Chizh, *Dostoevsky kak psikhopatalog* (Moscow, 1885), p. 60.
32 Erwin Stengel, *Suicide and Attempted Suicide* (New York, 1974), p. 53.
33 Alred Alvarez, *The Savage God. A Study of Suicide* (London, 1972), p. 107.
34 *Ibid.*, pp. 107-08.
35 Albert Camus, *The Myth of Sisyphus* (London, 1955), p. 86.
36 Fyodor Dostoyevsky, *The Possessed*, p. 61.
37 *Ibid.*, pp. 62-63.
38 *Ibid.*, pp. 688-89.
39 *Ibid.*, p. 689.
40 *Ibid.*, p. 221.
41 *Ibid.*, p. 272.
42 *Ibid.*, p. 253.
43 *Ibid.*, p. 688.
44 *Ibid.*, p. 266.
45 Konstantin Mochulsky, p. 429.
46 F.M. Dostoevsky, *Polnoe sobranie*, vol. 11, p. 131.
47 *Ibid.*, p. 132.
48 *Ibid.*, p. 133.
49 *Ibid.*, p. 175.
50 Richard Peace, *Dostoevsky. An Examination of the Major Novels* (Cambridge, 1971), p. 211.
51 Edward Wasiolek, p. 132.
52 Iu. G. Kudriavtsev, *Tri kruga Dostoevskogo* (Moscow, 1979), p. 192.
53 Richard Peace, p. 210.
54 Fyodor Dostoyevsky, *The Possessed*, p. 714.
55 E.H. Carr, *Dostoevsky. 1821-1881* (London, 1962), pp. 175-76.
56 Sergei Bobrov, "Ia Nikolai Stavrogin," *Krasnaia nov'*, 1922, no. 2, p. 336.
57 Yuri Glazov, " 'The Devils' by Dostoevsky and the Russian Intelligentsia," *Studies in Soviet Thought*, 17 (1977), p. 325.
58 Fyodor Dostoyevsky, *The Possessed*, p. 345.
59 *Ibid.*, p. 346.
60 *Ibid.*
61 *Ibid.*
62 *Ibid.*, p. 683.
63 F.M. Dostoevsky, *Polnoe sobranie*, vol. 11, p. 68.

5. A Raw Youth

1 Fyodor Dostoyevsky, *A Raw Youth*, translated by Constance Garnett (New York, 1961), p. 73.
2 *Ibid.*, p. 75.
3 *Ibid.*, p. 86.
4 *Ibid.*, p. 75.
5 I.I. Lapshin, "Obrazovanie tipa Krafta v 'Podrostke,' " in A.L. Bem, ed., *O Dostoevskom. Sbornik statei*, vol. 1 (Praha, 1929), pp. 140-44.
6 *Ibid.*, p. 141.
7 *Grazhdanin*, no. 19, May 7, 1873, quoted in F.M. Dostoevsky, *Polnoe sobranie sochineii v tridtsati tomakh*, vol. 17 (Leningrad, 1976), p. 261.
8 V.P. Meshchersky, "Tri sluchaia samoubiistva," *Grazhdanin*, no. 23, 1873, quoted in F.M. Dostoevsky, *Polnoe sobranie*, vol. 17, p. 261.

[9] F.M. Dostoevsky, *Polnoe sobranie*, vol. 16 (Leningrad, 1976), p. 76.
[10] *Ibid.*, p. 77.
[11] *Ibid.*, p. 76.
[12] *Ibid.*, p. 69.
[13] Fyodor Dostoyevsky, *A Raw Youth*, p. 189.
[14] *Ibid.*, p. 203.
[15] Emile Durkheim, *Suicide. A Study in Sociology* (New York, 1965), p. 15.
[16] Fyodor Dostoyevsky, *A Raw Youth*, p. 208.
[17] *Ibid.*
[18] *Ibid.*, p. 189.
[19] *Ibid.*, p. 420.
[20] *Ibid.*, p. 431.
[21] *Ibid.*, p. 421.
[22] *Ibid.*, p. 594.
[23] F.M. Dostoevsky, *Polnoe sobranie*, vol. 16, pp. 43 and 48.
[24] *Ibid.*, pp. 22-23 and 52.
[25] *Ibid.*, p. 163.
[26] Konstantin Mochulsky, *Dostoevsky. His Life and Work*, translated by Michael A. Minihan (Princeton, N.J., 1971), pp. 499-500.
[27] F.M. Dostoevsky, *Polnoe sobranie*, vol. 16, pp. 122, 141, and 346.
[28] *Ibid.*, pp. 223, 240, 293, 353 and 364.
[29] *Ibid.*, vol. 13, p. 246.
[30] *Ibid.*, vol. 16, p. 125.

6. The Brothers Karamazov

[1] R.L. Belknap suggests that "Smerdjakov initiates chains of events as a 'motiveless malignity', while Alesa stands at the end of the chain of events absorbing stimuli of all sorts, but starting no actions except perhaps with the boys." See Robert L. Belknap, *The Structure of "The Brothers Karamazov"* (The Hague-Paris, 1967), p. 72.
[2] Fyodor Dostoyevsky, *The Brothers Karamazov*, translated by David Magarshack (Harmondsworth, 1963), p. 262.
[3] *Ibid.*
[4] *Ibid.*, p. 724.
[5] F.M. Dostoevsky, *Polnoe sobranie sochinenii v tridtsati tomakh*, vol. 16 (Leningrad, 1976), pp. 137-38 and 179.
[6] *Ibid.*, vol. 15, p. 212.
[7] Fyodor Dostoyevsky, *The Brothers Karamazov*, p. 871.
[8] *Ibid.*, p. 833.
[9] *Ibid.*, p. 834.
[10] *Ibid.*, p. 884.
[11] N.M. Chirkov, *O stile Dostoevskogo* (Moscow, 1967), p. 238.
[12] Fyodor Dostoyevsky, *The Brothers Karamazov*, p. 741.
[13] *Ibid.*, pp. 731-32.
[14] E.I. Kiiko, "Iz istorii sozdaniia 'Brat'ev Karamazovykh' (Ivan i Smerdiakov)," in *Dostoevsky. Materialy i issledovaniia*, vol. 2 (Leningrad, 1976), p. 129.
[15] Fyodor Dostoyevsky, *The Brothers Karamazov*, p. 693.
[16] Edward Wasiolek, *Dostoevsky. The Major Fiction* (Cambridge, Mass., 1971), p. 176.
[17] Fyodor Dostoyevsky, *The Brothers Karamazov*, p. 730.
[18] *Ibid.*, p. 743.
[19] *Ibid.*, p. 732.

20 Edward Wasiolek, p. 172.

21 S.I. Gessen, "Tragediia dobra v 'Brat'iakh Karamazovykh' Dostoevskogo," in D. Fanger, ed., *O Dostoevskom. Stat'i* (Providence, Rhode Island, 1966), p. 227.

22 Fyodor Dostoyevsky, *The Brothers Karamazov*, p. 840.

23 *Ibid.*

24 F.M. Dostoevsky, *Polnoe sobranie*, vol. 15, pp. 353-54.

25 *Ibid.*, p. 356.

26 *Ibid.*, p. 365

27 E.I. Kiiko, pp. 125-29.

28 Alexandra H. Lyngstad, *Dostoevskij and Schiller* (The Hague-Paris, 1975), p. 56.

29 J.Ch.F. von Schiller, *Schillers Werke. Nationalausgabe*, vol. 3 (Weimar, 1953), p. 126.

30 George Steiner, *Tolstoy or Dostoevsky* (London, 1967), p. 278.

31 St. Matthew, 26-27. *The Bible. Authorized Version* (London, n.d.), pp. 797-98. Another account implies that the attempt of Judas to end his life by hanging himself failed and that he died from being disembowelled. See "The Acts of the Apostles," 1.18, *Ibid.*, p. 877.

32 Fyodor Dostoyevsky, *The Brothers Karamazov*, p. 743.

33 Richard Peace, *Dostoyevsky. An Examination of His Major Novels* (Cambridge, 1971), p. 263.

34 Karl A. Menninger, *Man Against Himself* (New York, 1938), p. 50.

35 *Ibid.*, pp. 24-83.

36 Norman L. Farberow and Edwin S. Shneidman, eds., *The Cry for Help* (New York, 1965), p. 301.

37 *Ibid.*, p. 298.

38 Ernest Jones, *Sigmund Freud. Life and Work*, vol. 2 (London, 1955), p. 315.

39 *The Cry for Help*, pp. 299-300.

40 D.J. West, *Murder Followed by Suicide* (Cambridge, Mass., 1967) p. 1.

41 *Ibid.*, p. 4.

42 Fyodor Dostoyevsky, *The Brothers Karamazov*, p. 175.

43 *Ibid.*, p. 686.

44 *Ibid.*, p. 687.

45 *Ibid.*, p. 474.

46 *Ibid.*, p. 485.

IV. THE DIARY OF A WRITER

1 At first Dostoevsky refers to her as to a "young girl of twenty-three or twenty-four," (see Feodor Dostoievsky, *The Diary of a Writer*, translated and annotated by Boris Brasol, vol. 1/New York, 1949/, p. 469); later, however, he admits his mistake and corrects himself by pointing out that she was only seventeen, (see *The Diary*, vol. 1, p. 546).

2 See L. Grossman, *Dostoevsky*, 2nd ed., corrected and appended (Moscow, 1965), p. 513.

3 *The Diary*, vol. 2, p. 592.

4 *Ibid.*, p. 866.

5 *Ibid.*, p. 860.

6 *Ibid.*, vol. 1, p. 336.

7 *Ibid.*

8 F.M. Dostoevsky, *Polnoe sobranie khudozhestvennykh proizvedenii. Dnevnik pisatelia*, vol. 11 (Moscow-Leningrad, 1929), p. 304.

9 F.M. Dostoevsky, *Pis'ma. 1872-1877*, vol. 3, edited and with commentaries by A.S. Dolinin (Moscow-Leningrad, 1934), pp. 213-14.

[10] *The Diary*, vol. 1, pp. 468-70.
[11] *Ibid.*, p. 469.
[12] *Ibid.*, p. 546.
[13] *Ibid.*, p. 547.
[14] *Ibid.*, p. 470.
[15] *Ibid.*
[16] *Ibid.*
[17] *Ibid.*, pp. 490-527.
[18] *Ibid.*, p. 524.
[19] Robert Louis Jackson, *The Art of Dostoevsky. Deliriums and Nocturnes* (Princeton, N.J., 1981), p. 246.
[20] E. Gashkene-Chervinskene, " 'Krotkaia' F. Dostoevskogo," *Nauchnye trudy vysshikh uchebnykh zavedenii Litovsckoi SSSR, Literatura*, XVI (2), (Vilnius, 1975), p. 41.
[21] R.L. Jackson, p. 247.
[22] *The Diary*, vol. 1, p. 535.
[23] *Ibid.*, p. 471.
[24] *Ibid.*
[25] *Ibid.*, pp. 472-73.
[26] V.A. Svitel'skii, "Kompozitsiia kak odno iz sredstv vyrazheniia avtorskoi otsenki v proizvedeniiakh Dostoevskogo," in *Doestoevsky. Materialy i issledovaniia*, vol. 2 (Leningrad, 1976), p. 14.
[27] Albert Camus, *The Myth of Sisyphus*, translated from the French by Justin O'Brien (London, 1955), p. 57.
[28] *Ibid.*, p. 91.
[29] *The Diary*, vol. 1, p. 470.
[30] *Ibid.*, p. 538.
[31] *Ibid.*, p. 540.
[32] *Ibid.*, p. 542.
[33] *Ibid.*, pp. 535-47.
[34] *Ibid.*, vol. 2, p. 689.
[35] Edward Wasiolek, *Dostoevsky. The Major Fiction* (Cambridge, Mass., 1971), p. 146.
[36] Konstantin Mochulsky, *Dostoevsky. His Life and Work*, translated by Michael A. Minihan (Princeton, N.J., 1971), p. 555.
[37] E. Wasiolek, p. 145.
[38] *Ibid.*, pp. 146-47.
[39] R.L. Jackson, p. 275.
[40] *Ibid.*, p. 17.

CONCLUSION

[1] Ronald William Maris, *Pathways to Suicide* (Baltimore, 1981), p. XVII.
[2] Edwin S. Shneidman, and others, compilers, *The Psychology of Suicide* (New York, 1970), p. 582.
[3] *Ibid.*, p. 128.

APPENDIX II
Suicide Notes

[1] Charles E. Osgood and Evelyn G. Walker, "Motivation and Language Behavior: A Content Analysis of Suicide Notes," *The Journal of Abnormal and Social*

Psychology, 1959, vol. 59, p. 67.

2 Feodor Dostoevsky, *Crime and Punishment*, translated by Jessie Coulson. Edited by George Gibian (New York, 1964), pp. 490-509.

3 Fyodor Dostoyevsky, *The Idiot*, translated by David Magarshack (Harmonds—worth, 1961), pp. 425-54.

4 Fyodor Dostoyevsky, *The Possessed*, translated by Constance Garnett (New York, 1961), pp. 636-37.

5 *Ibid.*, p. 690.

6 *Ibid.*, p. 345.

7 Fyodor Dostoyevsky, *A Raw Youth*, translated by Constance Garnett (New York, 1961), p. 189.

8 *Ibid.*, p. 208.

9 Fyodor Dostoyevsky, *The Brothers Karamazov*, translated by David Magarshack (Harmondsworth, 1963), p. 766.

10 *Ibid.*, p. 474.

11 Feodor Dostoievsky, *The Diary of a Writer*, translated and annotated by Boris Brasol, vol. 1 (New York, 1949), pp. 336-37.

12 *Ibid.*, p. 469.

13 *Ibid.*, p. 526.

14 *Ibid.*, vol. 2, p. 860.

SELECTED BIBLIOGRAPHY

Since it would be impossible to give, within the limited scope of this study, an exhaustive list of monographs and articles, dealing with the work and life of Dostoevsky, this bibliography is limited to the most essential primary sources and works of literary criticism used in the course of preparing this study. An additional section is devoted to monographs dealing with the problems of suicide.

PRIMARY SOURCES

Dostoevskaia, A.G. *Vospominaniia*. Moscow, 1971.

Dostoevsky, F.M. *Pis'ma. 1832-1881*. Edited and with commentaries by A.S. Dolinin. 4 vols. Moscow, 1928-1959.

----------. *Polnoe sobranie khudozhestvennykh proizvedenii*. 13 vols. Moscow-Leningrad, 1926-1930.

----------. *Polnoe sobranie khudozhestvennykh proizvedenii v tridtsati tomakh*. vols. 1-23. Leningrad, 1972-1981.

Dostoevsky, Fyodor. *The Notebooks for "Crime and Punishment."* Edited and translated by Edward Wasiolek. Chicago, 1967.

----------. *The Notebooks for "The Idiot."* Edited by Edward Wasiolek. Translated by Katharine Strelsky. Chicago, 1973.

Dostoievsky, Feodor. *The Diary of a Writer*. Translated and annotated by Boris Brasol. 2 vols. New York, 1949.

LITERARY CRITICISM

Belknap, Robert L. *The Structure of "The Brothers Karamazov."* The Hague-Paris, 1967.

Bem, A.L. *Dostoevsky. Psikhoanaliticheskie etiudy*. Praga, 1938.

Berdyaev, Nicholas. *Dostoevsky*. Translated by Donald Attwater. Cleveland, 1969.

Carr, E.H. *Dostoevsky. 1821-1881*. London, 1962.

Chirkov, N.M. *O stile Dostoevskogo*. Moscow 1963 and 1967.

Dostoevsky, F.M. *Materialy i issledovania*. Edited by A.S. Dolinin. Leningrad, 1935.

Dostoevsky i ego vremia. Edited by V.G. Bazanov and G.M. Fridlender. Leningrad, 1971.

Dostoevsky - khudozhnik i myslitel'. Sbornik statei. Moscow, 1972.
Dostoevsky. Materialy i issledovaniia. Vols. 1-4. Leningrad, 1974-1980.
Fanger, D., ed. *O Dostoevskom. Stat'i.* Providence, Rhode Island, 1966.
Frank, Joseph. *Dostoevsky. The Seeds of Revolt, 1821-1849.* Princeton, N.J., 1979.
Fridlender, G.M. *Realizm Dostoevskogo.* Moscow-Leningrad, 1964.
Gide, André. *Dostoevsky.* New York, 1967.
Grossman, L. *Dostoevsky.* 2nd edition, corrected and appended. Moscow, 1965.
Gus, M. *Idei i obrazy F.M. Dostoevskogo.* Moscow, 1971.
Ivanov, Vyacheslav. *Freedom and the Tragic Life. A Study in Dostoevsky.* New York, 1968.
Jackson, Robert Louis. *The Art of Dostoevsky. Deliriums and Nocturnes.* Princeton, N.J., 1981.
Kirpotin, V. Ia., *Razocharovanie i krushenie Rodiona Raskol'nikova.* Moscow, 1972.
Kudriavtsev, Iu.G. *Tri kruga Dostoevskogo.* Moscow, 1979.
Mochulsky, Konstantin. *Dostoevsky. His Life and Work.* Translated by Michael A. Minihan. Princeton, N.J., 1971.
Peace, Richard. *Dostoevsky. An Examination of the Major Novels.* Cambridge, 1971.
Steiner, George. *Tolstoy or Dostoevsky.* London, 1967.
Wasiolek, Edward. *Dostoevsky. The Major Fiction.* Cambridge, Mass., 1971.
Wellek, René, ed. *Dostoevsky. A Collection of Critical Essays.* Englewood Cliffs, N.J., 1962.

PROBLEMS OF SUICIDE

Alvarez, Alfred. *The Savage God. A Study of Suicide.* London, 1962.
Choron, Jaques. *Suicide.* New York, 1972.
Durkheim, Emile. *Suicide. A Study in Sociology.* Translated by John A. Spaulding and G. Simpson. New York, 1965.
Farberow, Norman L. and Edwin S. Shneidman, eds. *The Cry for Help.* New York, 1965.
Freud, Sigmund. *Standard Edition of Complete Psychological Works.* Vols. 11 and 23. London, 1957 and 1964.
Masaryk, Thomas G. *Suicide and the Meaning of Civilization.* Translated by W.G. Weist and R.G. Batson. Chicago, 1970.
Menninger, Karl A. *Man Against Himself.* New York, 1938.
Shneidman, Edwin S. and others, compilers. *The Psychology of Suicide.* New York, 1970.
Stengel, Erwin. *Suicide and Attempted Suicide.* New York, 1974.

INDEX